A waiter walks up to a table of four
Jewish women at the end of their meal...
"So, ladies, was anything OK?"

Published in the United States by Clarkson Potter/Publishers, an imprint of the
Crown Publishing Group, a division of Penguin Random House LLC, New York

crownpublishing.com
clarksonpotter.com

CLARKSON POTTER is a trademark and POTTER with colophon is a registered
trademark of Penguin Random House LLC.

Originally published by Mitchell Beazley, a division of Octopus Publishing Group Ltd,
Great Britain, in 2016

Grateful acknowledgment is made to Penguin Random House LLC for permission to
reprint an excerpt from *The New Book of Middle Eastern Food* by Claudia Roden,
copyright © 1968, 1972, 1985, 2000 by Claudia Roden. Used by permission of Alfred
A. Knopf, an imprint of the Knopf Doubleday Publishing Group, a division of Penguin
Random House LLC. All rights reserved.

Library of Congress Cataloguing-in-Publication is available upon request.

ISBN 978-0-451-49661-4
eBook ISBN 978-0-451-49662-1

Printed in China

Book design by Octopus Publishing Group Ltd
Jacket design by Here Design
Jacket photographs by Helen Cathcart

10 9 8 7 6 5 4 3 2 1
First U.S. Edition

THE

Palomar

COOKBOOK

MODERN ISRAELI CUISINE

LAYO PASKIN AND TOMER AMEDI

Photography by Helen Cathcart

Clarkson Potter/Publishers
NEW YORK

AN INTRODUCTION
by Layo Paskin

In this house, we're all mongrels, second- and third-generation immigrants who have adopted London and are united by our passion for food: food as the essence of our identities, our culture, our everyday lives and our celebrations. We cherish the recipes of generations hailing from Southern Europe, North Africa, the Near East and the Levant, and blend these flavors of home and history with the distinctive verve and vibrancy of modern cooking. For all of us, food tells stories, of where we are from and where we're going, and the narrative begins fortuitously at our grandmothers' heels.

So we start at home, watching and learning from the way our families adapt to new communities by combining the fundamentals of their own culture with the best of what they encounter. We have applied this adaptable, acquisitive approach to the innovation and energy of our restaurant. With this cookbook we come very naturally full circle back to the home. We were determined that our book should be brimming with recipes that not only reflect The Palomar restaurant experience but that are easy, fun, quick and simple to create, always beautiful to look at and utterly delicious to eat.

What has brought such pleasure in the restaurant is our play on associations and memories, our rootedness in land and history and our encounters with the new and modern, and we want you to have fun in the same way at home, too. We converge at an irreverent meeting point between the very best of our collective cultures and we invite you, our home cooks, to join us there.

Tomer has written the recipes, Papi tells his own story through food, Yael reveals her love of all things created from flour, Zoe shares a glimpse into a day in our lives and Marco demonstrates his passion for the art of the cocktail. Welcome to our world. The Palomar is an open kitchen, a pressure cooker where all is visible, a dropped pot, a burned hand, an unstoppable swear word, a look from Kitchen to Floor. We adapt and work to this rhythm, always unfolding, genuine, warm, engaging, professional and honest — and all underpinned by our DNA of hospitality. The Palomar is our heritage with a twist; modernity with lasting style.

_____ **Cooking in the Middle East is deeply traditional and nonintellectual — an inherited art.**
Claudia Roden

THE COLLECTOR AND THE TRAVELER
— WHY THE PALOMAR?

There's something beautifully timeless about the word, and it felt right as soon as I said it out loud. The word "palomar" originates from the period of Spanish rule in California, from the end of the 17th to the early 19th centuries, and means "dovecote," a bird house specifically intended for pigeons or doves. Dovecotes are to be found throughout the geographical regions of our cuisine, particularly in the Eastern Mediterranean and the Middle East. The oldest date back thousands of years and are thought to have been common in Ancient Egypt and Iran. We wanted a name that was evocative and said something of the past; classic and romantic yet also strong and enduring.

So, with the name decided, we prepared a brief for our architect, Christian Ducker of Gundry & Ducker, from which he worked with the phrase "the collector and the traveler" in mind — immigrants on a journey. As with any design, you have to work with the space available to you and with every constraint and freedom that it offers. We had to use every last inch of our space to make it work! The design is inspired by the golden age of travel (see above), the idea that our food is drawn from a variety of regions and cultures and brought together in one place, a mix of all our backgrounds and heritage. At this stage we approached Here Design, which took this brief and followed through with the look and feel of The Palomar, from the wonderful calligraphy in our name created by looking back at artwork of the period, to the color palette, through to every detail of the design, from menus to coasters, napkins to cocktail sticks. Detail, detail, detail.

RUPERT STREET

Perhaps if you look across from somewhere like Hampstead Heath can you imagine a London that was once a small city surrounded by farmland and villages? As it grew, these merged and slowly London became the great metropolis it is today. Soho, originally known as St. Giles Field, was the hunting ground and a royal park for Henry VIII in the 16th century. A hundred years later it was granted to Henry Jermyn, 1st Earl of St. Albans, and renamed Soho Fields; he in turn leased it to Richard Frith — the former having the famous street in St. James's and the latter the street in Soho named after them. Pressure from a growing population and subsequent development of the city (sound familiar?) meant that Soho expanded. It became a home for the fleeing Huguenots and by the mid-1700s was renowned for its music halls, drinking dens, theaters and prostitutes. Its bohemian reputation, one that I rather admire, continued to flourish throughout the 20th century, when it was established as a center for artists, musicians, writers, the sex and film industries, private clubs and, of course, restaurants.

First mentioned in 1677, Rupert Street was evidently named after Prince Rupert and existed then, as now, on the fringes. The buildings that line the street today are more recent in origin, dating from around 1880. Number 34, where our restaurant resides, was originally a boarding house for dressmakers, vintners and wheelwrights. Although we considered several other sites in London, Soho has always been a home from home for me, and it took little persuasion for the others to agree that it is the perfect location for The Palomar.

WHAT'S IN
THE PANTRY?

———

The best place to start? For me, it's got to be the pantry. I have to admit that I'm something of a pantry voyeur; you can tell so much about people and their culture by having a good rummage through their kitchen cabinets. As a kid with a growing interest in cooking, this was the first place I looked in a new friend's house. There are always interesting ingredients to discover in someone's pantry, and it provides an immediate insight into the basics of their cooking culture.

The Palomar pantry and my home pantry are pretty much the same; there you'll find pomegranate molasses alongside rice vinegar, freekeh and risotto rice, a collage of ingredients with a strong Middle Eastern inflection, my interpretation of the old and the new.

The truth is, equipping your pantry is much easier than it seems, especially now that you can get anything and everything online. We do live in exciting times. Most of the ingredients will last a long time, and even if you're cooking on a daily basis, you might only have to stock up a maximum of two or three times a year — not a huge task. I strongly recommend doing one big stock-up rather than trying to source individual items for each recipe. It will make your life easier and take your daily cooking experience to a whole new level.

by Tomer Amedi

Dry Stores

I've assembled the following short glossary of ingredients that will help with many of the following recipes. This is the ideal way to begin getting to grips with the staples of a new cuisine.

Freekeh

Simply put, freekeh is smoked green wheat. The wheat is picked while still young and moist, then piled up and set on fire; the end result is a herbal, smoky cereal that is way more fun to cook with than regular wheat. To this day, the Druze, an esoteric religious community living in the Galilee area, still use the old-school methods of production (it's even mentioned in the Bible!), and it's an important ingredient not only in Galilean cooking but also in Lebanese, Syrian and Egyptian. It's easy to cook with — you just need the right amount of liquid and some love and attention.

Bulgur wheat

Bulgur is wheat (usually durum) that has been precooked, then dried and cracked. It became popular in the Middle East thanks to the influence of the Ottoman Empire. The wheat is cracked to three different particle sizes — coarse, fine and *jarish* (extra fine) — and each size is good for a different use, for example in kibbeh, tabbouleh, Kubenia (see p.99) and so on. It's also versatile in that it can be served hot or cold. But the best thing about bulgur is that it's super-easy to cook with — no actual cooking is needed, just a soak in boiled water, salt and a touch of oil.

Pomegranate molasses

This thick, dark, rich, sour and tangy liquid is a big star in Persian cuisine and it is one of my favorite ingredients. Basically it's a reduction of pomegranate juice so the flavors are really concentrated. We use it in the restaurant for stews, vinaigrettes, vegetables and even in desserts.

Date syrup

This date honey, also called date molasses, has a great natural sweetness and a loose texture. It's good not only for desserts or as a substitute for honey but for vinaigrettes and savory dishes, too. My papa likes to mix it with raw tahini and spread it on toast for breakfast. He's smart, my old man.

Tahini

The king of pastes and a mega-key ingredient in Middle Eastern cooking, tahini is made from ground sesame seeds. The quality of the tahini is determined by whether the sesame seeds are unhulled or hulled, toasted or not, and the method used to grind them, for example stoneground. For me, a good tahini should be nutty and smooth with a hint of sweetness. Mightily versatile, tahini is great in so many kinds of dishes, savory and sweet, raw or cooked, and it's very easy to handle. Good brands to look for are Al Nakhil, Al Arz and Al Taj.

Israeli couscous

Called *ptitim* in Hebrew, this is basically a flour- and water-based baked pasta. The story behind this awesome ingredient goes all the way back to the austerity period in Israel (1949–56), when times were hard and the first Prime Minister of Israel, David Ben-Gurion, approached the biggest food company at that time, Osem, and said: "Guys, I need a tasty, easy, cheap, kick-ass fast-food solution, so go to your labs and bring me the holy grail!" (Well, I'm not sure those were his exact words, but that was the spirit of them — he was a cool prime minister, they say.) So they came up with this form of pasta shaped to look like rice, which to this day is known as "Ben-Gurion Rice" by the people of Israel. The famous couscous shape was to come later. Every child in Israel (present company included) grew up on this super-easy-to-cook ingredient, and I can only recommend you do the same for your kids. But wait, the story doesn't end here! In the late 1990s, a couple of New York chefs started to use Israeli couscous and now it can be widely found in Michelin-starred restaurants. A humble beginning with a superstar ending, this is a Cinderella story come true.

Kosher salt

"So does the Rabbi bless this salt or something?" "How does it become kosher?" and many more questions are frequently asked of me about this ingredient, and all because it's been wrongly named! It should actually be called koshering salt, given that it has a much larger grain size than ordinary table salt and is a purer form (no iodine is added). In Judaism, meat must be drained of blood and koshering salt is used for the purpose because its larger, purer grain helps to draw the blood more effectively, which is how it got its name. In this book, as in our restaurant, when I refer to salt I always mean kosher salt (unless Maldon salt is specified), so do make the effort to find it to replace your regular table salt — you won't regret it. You can, however, use regular table salt for all the recipes if you prefer, but you will need to reduce the quantities given, as table salt is denser (it delivers more actual salt per measure), or simply salt to taste.

Rose water

The name pretty much says it all — this is water flavored with rose petals, used frequently in Middle Eastern desserts as well as in Pakistani cooking, and the Persians add it to their lemonade. It is a key ingredient in our Malabi (see p.206).

Orange blossom water

Maa zaher in Arabic, this is another amazingly flavorful flower essence with a very refreshing scent. Genuine orange blossom water is alcohol-free and is used mostly in Moroccan and Algerian desserts for making baklava and flavored syrups, but we create a killer ice cream with it (see p.199). Don't be afraid to experiment, though, as you can use both this and rose water as you would vanilla extract, for example.

Spices

I could write a whole book on spices — and that's just about their history. Nowadays we take for granted the little packets that we see in the supermarket filled with seeds, tree bark or dried leaves. But just consider that spice trading dates way back to 2000BC, and once upon a time, long before oil, black pepper was known as "black gold." Spices carved history and built empires; they were central to the discovery of new worlds and caused wars along the way. They were also used as the earliest medicines, and of course traditional Chinese medicine is predicated on the use of herbs and spices. And if that's not enough spice for you, just cast a glance at the perfume and cosmetics industries. Spices are everywhere.

But this is a cookbook, not a history lesson, so let's get back to the reason we're here. Spices are the dried forms of vegetables, fruits, seeds, bark or flowers used for flavoring, coloring or preserving food. In other words, spices are my life! The spice shops of Machane Yehuda market in Jerusalem perfume my memories of the days long before I started cooking. There are maybe eight to ten spice shops, each one with its own special spice mixes and personality. And wow, the smell of those piles of paprika and cumin, turmeric and cinnamon, which you buy by weight according to how much you want, is so intoxicating, so exotic.

In general, I recommend buying any spice that comes as a seed in its original form rather than ground. While most spices lose their fragrance once ground, the aroma is intensified when whole spices are heated due to the oil they contain, so it's infinitely better to prepare your own ground spices. Simply toast the whole spices in a dry pan over a medium heat and then grind in a coffee or spice grinder, or use a pestle and mortar — you won't believe the difference, and your kitchen will smell like a spice shop straight away.

So which are the spices we use at The Palomar and are destined to become staples of your pantry?

Cumin seeds

One of the biggest stars in our kitchen, cumin has a powerful and earthy aroma. I use it as a base for a lot of our spice mixes (see p.18 and 20).

Coriander seeds

These are the dried fruits of the coriander plant, whose fresh leaves, stems and roots are also widely used as an herb in Middle Eastern cuisine. The green coriander seeds have a lemony, nutty flavor and can be used fresh — crushed or pulverized — in salads, cooked food and even desserts. Jams and marmalades are greatly enhanced by them too.

Paprika

This vibrant spice comes from the air-dried fruits of the chile pepper family. It is available in a couple of different forms (dry or with oil) and in heat levels (sweet or hot) or smoked. I prefer the Moroccan sweet paprika, which is mixed with a little oil (my mother's Moroccan, and I'm a mama's boy, what can I do?).

Turmeric

Ground turmeric comes from a root (or rhizome) in the ginger family, which is boiled rather than baked, dried and then pulverized to a powder. It has a bright yellow color with a slight bitterness, and is a key ingredient in our Jerusalem and Hawaij Spice Mixes (see p.18 and 20).

Cardamom

This small green pod with black seeds inside comes from a plant that grows mainly in India and Pakistan. It's a central ingredient in a lot of our spice mixes but also used for flavoring sweets, teas and coffee.

Star anise

This star-shaped spice is actually the fruit of a tree in its dried form and is widely used in Chinese and Indian cuisine, but I also value it because it has the anise accent of arak (an anise-flavored spirit) and fennel.

Fennel seeds

The seeds of the well-known fennel plant have a mild sweetness and a delicate anise flavor. We use them a lot with fish and seafood (but not exclusively). Try infusing them in your tea — great for calming your tummy after a big feast.

Za'atar

Za'atar is a dried leafy herb from the oregano family, and as with oregano, it is used both fresh and dried. It is one of the ingredients in Za'atar Spice Mix (at least the sort I prefer) along with sumac, sesame seeds and dried thyme (see p.20). The mix is often used to season Labneh cheese (see p.41) and salads.

Dried rose petals

Along with rose water, these often feature in Middle Eastern desserts, but not solely — I also use them in spice mixes to give them extra aroma (see right).

Mahlab

This spice (often sold as mahlep or mahleb) is made from Mahlab cherry pits, and has a bitter almond-like taste. It is used mainly for desserts and in baking.

Sumac

Made from the red buds of a bush that grows in subtropical and temperate regions, sumac has a tangy, sour taste. It is widely used in Middle Eastern cooking, and is a key component of my Za'atar Spice Mix (see p.20). In the past, sumac buds were used in the leather industry to soften up hides, as they have a high tannin content.

Dried limes

Limoo amani, to give them their Persian name, are limes that have been left to dry in the sun. These guys are little citrus explosions, delivering an intense lemony hit. I like to add them to stews, but you can also grind them and add them to legumes and grains. Make sure you give them a small puncturing poke before you add them whole, to release their flavor.

Spice Mixes

Spice mixes are another great way to get acquainted with a new cuisine. They're like smelling the very essence of the kitchen in one sniff; magic powders that can transport you straight to Morocco, Yemen or India. They are also a great way to ensure that you use the spices in their freshest and most vibrant form, and hit the right combination of flavors every time.

For all the recipes the method is the same: simply toast the seeds for 2–3 minutes in a dry pan over a medium heat, then grind them finely in a coffee or spice grinder, or use a pestle and mortar. Keep in an airtight container and store in a dark place (like a pantry or larder). I prefer to make them in small amounts, as it's best to use the mixes as fresh as possible, keeping them for 1–2 months max.

Ras el hanout spice mix

Meaning "top of the shop," this North African spice mix is the best a spice shop owner has to offer you. The recipe is usually kept secret but can contain up to 17 different spices, and varies according to whether it's to be used with lamb, beef or fish and so on, as well as from shop to shop. This recipe is inspired by the one my mama uses for a chicken tagine with dried fruit, but in truth you can use it with any kind of meat.

* 5 tbsp sweet paprika
* 4 tbsp toasted cumin seeds or 2 tbsp ground cumin
* 1 tbsp dried rose petals
* 3 tbsp toasted coriander seeds
* 1 tsp ground cinnamon
* 2 tbsp black peppercorns or 1 tbsp cracked black peppercorns
* ½ tsp cloves

Jerusalem spice mix

This excellent spice mix was born in Jerusalem by mistake as a flavoring for an offal dish (see p.182). I really like it with chicken, but it's great with all kinds of meat and works brilliantly as a rub for grilling and other quick cooking methods.

* 2 tbsp ground turmeric
* 5 tbsp toasted coriander seeds
* 4 tbsp toasted cumin seeds
* 1 tsp cardamom pods (ditch the husks before you grind them)
* 1 tsp black peppercorns

Persian stew spice mix

This spice mix is inspired by a Persian dish called *khoreshet* (stew) *sabzi* (greens). We use it in the restaurant to prepare an oxtail dish (see p.158), but any slow-cooked stew or rice dish would be great with this mix.

* 2 tbsp ground turmeric
* 1 tbsp cardamom pods
* 1 tbsp whole cloves
* 5 tbsp toasted coriander seeds
* 5 tbsp toasted cumin seeds
* 1 tsp allspice berries (optional)
* 4 tbsp dried dill

Hawaij spice mix

This is one of my favorites, a Yemeni mix spice that's also very popular in Israel and has been embraced by many other cuisines in the region. When I cook with my mama and something is missing, she always says to me, "Add a bit of hawaij," and you know what, she's always right. I like to use is for stews, meatballs and kebabs — and the Yemenis make a killer beef shin soup with it. I even like to add some when I'm pickling. To be honest, I still like the hawaij I get from Machane Yehuda market the best, but this version is very close to the real thing.

* 4 tbsp black peppercorns or 2 tbsp cracked black peppercorns
* 4 tbsp toasted cumin seeds or 2 tbsp ground cumin
* 1 tbsp cardamom pods (ditch the husks before you grind them) or 1 tsp ground cardamom
* 2 tbsp ground turmeric
* 1 tsp cloves
* 2 tbsp toasted coriander seeds
* 2 tbsp dried cilantro

Baharat spice mix

A spice mix from the Arabic kitchen (the meaning of the word baharat is simply "spices"), there are quite a few versions around, as every region has its own recipe (you can find it in Iraqi, Syrian, Lebanese, Turkish, Kurdish and Israeli cooking). The one that I prefer goes well with all kinds of meat and stews, but my favorite way of using it is with lamb and chicken — it works really well as a rub for grilling or marinating. If you want to use it with fish, simply omit the cinnamon from the recipe.

* 4 tbsp sweet paprika
* 2 tbsp black peppercorns
* 1 tsp ground cinnamon
* 1 tsp cardamom pods
* 4 tbsp toasted cumin seeds
* 1 tsp grated nutmeg
* 2 tbsp toasted coriander seeds
* 1 tsp allspice berries
* 1 tsp whole cloves

Za'atar spice mix

You can buy really good za'atar spice mix these days, but for those of you who can't find one of these or want to go DIY, this is an easy recipe that comes close to the original.

* 4 tbsp sumac
* 4 tbsp dried thyme
* 2 tbsp dried oregano or za'atar
* 1 tsp Maldon salt flakes
* 1 tbsp toasted sesame seeds

Blitz all the ingredients except the sesame seeds in a coffee or spice grinder, or grind with a pestle and mortar, then stir in the toasted sesame seeds.

Preparing your own dried herbs

You can dry fresh thyme or oregano in the oven preheated to 300°F for 10 minutes.

Nuts

Nuts are great. In fact, I absolutely love them, and there are always at least three or four different kinds of nut in my home pantry at any given time. I know you expect to hear that the reason is because they're very healthy for you… yada yada yada. And indeed they are, but that's not the main reason why they're amazing. It's because they add so many layers to the food: taste, texture and flavor. When I'm missing an ingredient in a dish to make it perfect, 99% of the time that ingredient is a nut.

It's really important to toast nuts before adding them to a dish, first so that the oil they contain can be released and with it the aromas and flavors; second, so that their texture changes, since nuts are chewy before toasting; and third, so that we can salt them.

To toast nuts, I use their size as a guide, and group and treat them accordingly — the bigger they are, the lower the oven temperature and longer the toasting time. Besides the raw shelled nuts themselves, you will need a little canola oil and some salt.

Toasting pine nuts, pistachio nuts, hazelnuts and slivered almonds

1. Preheat the oven to 325°F.

2. Toss the nuts with a drizzle of canola oil and salt to taste in a mixing bowl.

3. Spread out on a baking sheet and toast for 7–10 minutes — we're looking for a golden brown color and an intoxicating nutty smell.

4. Remove from the oven and let cool, then store in an airtight container. They will keep fresh for up to 2 weeks.

Toasting Brazil nuts, walnuts and whole blanched almonds

1. Preheat the oven to 300°F.

2. Prepare the nuts for toasting as above, then toast for 10–15 minutes. Let cool and store in the same way.

Using toasted nuts

Once they are toasted, I use the nuts in three different forms: simply as they are (such as with pine nuts and slivered almonds); chopped; or ground — use a coffee or spice grinder, which we have already seen is great for grinding spices, or a small food processor or pestle and mortar.

THE MEAL
BEFORE THE MEAL

We all have our little rituals when it comes to big meals, whether it's a midweek get-together with friends, Sunday lunch or a big family occasion, and in every Israeli or Jewish household, mine included, Friday night dinner is the most important meal of the week. The family spruces up a little and gathers around the table, maybe with some guests. We bless the wine (or just drink it in my case) and the Challah bread. And then we address the eternal Friday night challenge: "How are we supposed to eat all that?"

In my family, we start the meal with at least eight or nine different mezzes. They're the cornerstone of my mama's kitchen, and any day of the week she'll have at least five or six stacked in the fridge, waiting for me to come at them with some bread. Everything from Spiced Olives with Rose Petals and Balsamic Vinegar (see p.42) and Chrain (see p.33) to Baba Ganoush (see p.51) and Matbucha (see p.52), it's a never-ending parade of colors and flavors, all freshly homemade with love.

Keeping a few mezzes in the fridge at any one time makes life so easy. Whether you want a quick snack, a sandwich or something to dip into over a beer with friends while you watch a movie or a match, they're ready to go. Many of the mezzes I'm going to teach you to make are important building blocks for more complex recipes later in the book, so I highly recommend that you try them out and get into the habit of storing them in your fridge as a matter of course. Staples such as Harissa (see p.27), Cured Lemons (see p.24) and Tapenade (see p.35) are so easy to do, require no real cooking and will hugely enrich your repertoire of dishes. You'll see what I mean once they become part of your routine.

by Tomer Amedi

Cured lemons

Makes 7 cups

First off, there is a difference between these tangy, intensely savory cured lemon slices and the more ubiquitous preserved lemons. Ours are cured in olive oil and salt, while the latter are suspended in brine. Switching water for oil eliminates entirely that bleach-y taste preserved lemons can carry. All over the Middle East you can buy the very best-quality cured and preserved lemons, but in London... less so. Once I settled in the UK, I was forced to conquer my reluctance to cure my own. For some reason, many people avoid doing it. Silly, really — it's not complicated and the result is far superior to anything you can buy. The only thing you need is a little patience. I can credit Papi with dispelling my curing fears, and frankly now I can never cure enough. Cured lemons, in slices and as a paste (see right), are an essential part of our cooking: chop the sliced lemons and add them to salads, sandwiches, stews and so on, while the paste version is great for all kinds of sauces or even just served with some bread or Pita (see p.229). To Papi, the curing process is a religious ritual — when the rest of the kitchen is in a frenzy, for Papi it's only: Board. Knife. Lemons.

* 10 unwaxed lemons, cut into slices ¼ inch thick (discard the end bits)
* ¼ cup Maldon salt
* ¾ cup canola oil
* ¾ cup olive oil

1. Sterilize a 7-cup airtight container or jar by simply pouring boiling water into it, then drying it thoroughly with a clean cloth, or putting it through a dishwasher can also do the job.

2. Arrange one layer of the lemon slices in the container or jar, then sprinkle with some of the salt. Repeat the process until all the lemon slices are used up, making sure not to fill the container or jar all the way to the top.

3. Cover with oil all the way to the top and seal with the airtight lid. The lemon slices will be ready to use after 3 days.

4. From here, there are 3 rules you have to follow (religiously!):

Rule 1 Like vampires, cured lemons don't like the sunlight, so always keep them in a cool, dark place.

Rule 2 Always make sure the lemons are fully covered with oil.

Rule 3 Always make sure you take your cured slices out of the container or jar with a clean utensil — we don't want the lemons to be contaminated.

5. The lemons can be kept somewhere cool and dry for up to a week, or for up to a month in the fridge.

* 1 recipe of Cured Lemons
  (see left)
* 1 tbsp sweet paprika
* ½ tsp crushed red pepper flakes
* 1 tsp toasted and ground
  cumin seeds

Cured lemon paste

Makes 4 cups

This is the final process after you have been so patient waiting for your lovely lemons to cure, and boy oh boy are you going to love the end result. This is the ultimate sour paste, and we use it in the restaurant for so many recipes that it has an honorary place along with salt and olive oil. Once you go paste, you never go back.

1. Strain the Cured Lemons from the oil and reserve the oil.

2. Place the lemons in a blender or food processor, add the spices and blend.

3. Then while you continue to blend, add the reserved oil gradually until you have a smooth paste — you should use around one-quarter to one-half of the oil.

4. Place the paste in a sterilized 5-cup airtight container or jar (see p.24). and cover with some of the remaining oil. The lemon paste can be kept in the fridge for up to 3 weeks. You can use the leftover oil for a salad dressing — you just need to make sure you balance it with some sugar/honey/date syrup etc.

Harissa

Makes 2¼ cups

Along with Cured Lemon Paste (see p.25), I can easily say this is one of the most common ingredients we use at The Palomar. This red, flavorful dried pepper paste is a key ingredient in North African cooking, the origin of which, so they say, is Tunisia, but I like the coarse Moroccan version better (don't tell the Tunisians). If you buy harissa ready-made, make sure you get a good-quality version — it should look coarser than a tomato purée (the Belazu version is delicious). I've added some dried rose petals to this recipe to give it a nice aroma.

* 1 cup dried sweet peppers (Mexican or Moroccan are perfect)
* 3–4 garlic cloves, peeled
* 2 tbsp crushed red pepper flakes or 3–4 dried hot chiles (the small ones are better for this recipe and of course, as always, if you like it hotter, add more)
* 1 tbsp toasted and ground cumin seeds
* 1 tsp toasted and ground coriander seeds
* ½ tsp toasted and ground caraway seeds (optional)
* 1 tbsp dried rose petals
* finely grated zest of 1 small unwaxed lemon
* salt, to taste
* ¾ cup canola oil
* ½ cup olive oil

1. Cut the tops off the peppers with scissors, then soak them in a bowl of cold water for 30 minutes until soft.

2. Strain and pat the peppers dry, then grind coarsely in a meat grinder (the one that comes with your electric mixer is excellent for this).

3. Pass the peppers through the grinder again, this time with the garlic, spices, rose petals, lemon zest and salt. If you don't have a grinder, you can use a food processor or a blender, but just make sure you blitz the mixture in short pulses and add a bit of the oil as you go so that it blends nice and easy. You want to retain a bit of a rough texture, so don't go crazy with the blitzing.

4. Place in a bowl, add most of both oils, saving some to cover the harissa afterward, and mix lightly with a whisk — the peppers will "drink" the oil with lots of love; they really love oil, so don't be shy.

5. Transfer to a sterilized 2¼-cup airtight container or jar (see p.24) and cover with the rest of the oil. The harissa can be kept in the fridge for up to 2 weeks, or freeze in small batches to use on future occasions. Don't be afraid to add extra canola oil every time you use any if it looks a bit dry — there's no such thing as too much oil for harissa, plus you can use any excess for dressings for oysters (see p.82).

White tahini sauce

Makes 2¼ cups

For a good tahini sauce, you need to start with a good tahini paste. Personally, I like Lebanese tahini, as it's rich and natural — the brand I use in the restaurant is Al Nakhil. Some like their tahini sauce with garlic, which I find overpowering; I like to really taste the sesame when I eat it. Tahini is really the Master Paste, as you can put it on almost anything and it will make it better. But my favorite tahini marriage is with bread or pita (see p.229). Any time of day or night is a good time to mop up some tahini with pita; so simple but so tasty.

Before you start, it's important to point out that every tahini paste is a bit different, so the volume of water needed will change from brand to brand. The good news is that, if you add the water slowly, you'll easily be able to judge when you've hit the right texture. And what is the right texture, you ask? It all depends how you like it! I like it to be somewhere in the middle so that when you dip a spoon and lift it, the tahini oozes down slowly. There's no right or wrong — some like it very runny (like my wife), some like it thick and dense (like my mama and papa) and me, I like it in the middle!

1. Spoon the tahini paste into a bowl, add the water gradually and beat constantly with a whisk. At first the tahini will become denser (don't panic!) and then it will start to loosen up. Stop when you hit the texture you like.

2. Add the lemon juice and salt to taste. You can keep the sauce refrigerated, tightly covered with plastic wrap, for up to 2 days (it gets a bit thicker in the fridge).

* 1 cup tahini paste
* ¾–1 cup ice-cold water
* ¼ cup freshly squeezed lemon juice
* salt, to taste

Velvet tomatoes

Serves 4

We serve this fresh tomato dip in the restaurant with our Kubaneh Bread (see p.230). Easy to make, it's a kind of a mix between a gazpacho and a Yemeni grated tomato sauce, and you can have it with bread or even as a cold fresh sauce for raw fish or some grilled vegetables — try it and decide for yourself. The most important thing is to get really good ripe tomatoes and extra virgin olive oil — there's no room to hide with only two key ingredients.

———

1. Put the tomatoes, chile and cumin into the most powerful blender you can get your hands on.

2. Blend until smooth. Then while continuing to blend, add the olive oil gradually. The mixture will emulsify and give you that velvety texture you want.

3. Add salt to taste, and then comes the most important part: strain through the finest sieve you have (in the restaurant we use a chinois), as we don't want any stray tomato skins. I prefer to enjoy this the same day, but it will keep fresh in a sterilized airtight container (see p.24) in the fridge for 2 days, or you can store it for up to 5 days and use in any sauces for pasta and other dishes.

* About 1 pound very good-quality red tomatoes (ripe and a bit soft are the best), cut into quarters
* ½–1 green chile (depending on how hot you like it)
* 1 tsp toasted and ground cumin seeds
* 4–5 tbsp extra virgin olive oil
* salt, to taste

Watercress pesto

Makes 1 cup

I came up with this recipe when we opened our Machneyuda restaurant in Jerusalem as one of the toppings for the Shakshukit (see p.156), and it has been with me ever since. It's a great pesto for sandwiches, pastas and even salad dressings, with a lovely balance between the bitterness of the watercress and the sweetness of the honey. It's a twist on the classic Italian recipe.

----

* 1 bunch of watercress, any really thick stems removed
* 1 bunch of basil, ditto
* 1½ tbsp toasted pine nuts (see p.21)
* ½ tsp honey
* 1½ tbsp grated Parmesan cheese (I like to use Parmigiano Reggiano, but Grana Padano will also do the trick)
* 1–2 garlic cloves, peeled
* 1 Garlic Confit Clove (see p.46), optional
* 2 tbsp freshly squeezed lemon juice
* ¼ cup olive oil, or more if needed, plus 2 tsp
* ¼ cup canola oil, ditto, plus 2 tsp
* salt, to taste

1. In a blender or food processor, blend all the ingredients and 2 tbsp of each oil until well combined. Then while continuing to blend, add another 2 tbsp of each oil gradually. Use a bit more oil if needed to get to a smoother texture (sometimes bunches of watercress are pretty chunky).

2. Transfer to a sterilized 1-cup airtight container or a jar (see p.24) and cover over with the extra 2 teaspoons of each oil, which will help the pesto to stay nicely green and fresh. In the restaurant we make this fresh on a daily basis, but you can keep it for 3–4 days in the fridge.

A general tip for storing pesto: the more Parmesan and oil you use in the recipe, the longer it will last.

Red onions & sumac

Serves 6

This is a great mezze on its own or an excellent add-on for any kind of grilled meat or fish. I'm a big fan of onions — raw, cooked or cured. The sumac and the lemon lightly cure the onions but still leave them with some punch: a perfect balance.

———

* 3 red onions, cut in half and thinly sliced
* large handful of chopped parsley
* 1 tsp toasted and ground coriander seeds
* 1 tbsp sumac
* 3 tbsp freshly squeezed lemon juice (about 1 lemon)
* ¼ cup olive oil
* salt, to taste

1. Mix all the ingredients together in a bowl and season to taste with salt.

2. Cover the bowl with plastic wrap and let rest in the fridge for at least an hour. It will keep in the fridge for up to 2 days.

Chrain

Spicy horseradish & beet

Makes 3½ cups

This spicy horseradish paste is the Ashkenazi Jewish answer to the Yemeni Schug (see p.34). It's traditionally eaten with gefilte fish (I know, those cold, gray, sweet poached fish balls — I still don't entirely get the appeal myself, but they taste pretty good if done properly), giving a great kick and balance to the sweetness of the fish. In fact, I think chrain makes all Ashkenazi food taste better. We serve it in the restaurant with Hand-chopped Chicken Liver (see p.45) and to me it can play the same role as mustard, so I also like to use it for sandwiches.

———

* 1 beet, skin on, boiled in water until soft
* 1 horseradish root, about 1lb, peeled and roughly chopped
* 1 tsp sugar
* 2 tbsp white wine vinegar
* ¼ cup canola or vegetable oil
* salt, to taste

Now, there are two schools when it comes to the texture of chrain, the grated school and the blended school. I'm of the blended school.

1. Drain the cooked beet and, once cool enough to handle, peel and then cut it up roughly.

2. Place all the ingredients except for half the oil in a powerful blender and blend on a high speed for a good 5 minutes; this is the hard part, as the horseradish will make you cry, but you are strong and I believe you can make it!

3. Transfer the mixture to a sterilized 1¾-pint airtight container or jar (see p.24) and cover with the rest of the oil. The chrain can be kept in the fridge for up to 2 weeks.

Schug

Yemeni chile & cilantro paste

Makes about 1 ¾ cups

When I was growing up, I didn't like spicy food. I can remember all my family at the Friday night dinner table debating as to whether the Moroccan burned green chile salad or the Yemini schug were spicy enough. Were the chiles that my papa had bought at the market hot as hell itself? And had my mama put enough of them in to make everyone cry? The more painful it was to eat, the happier it made everyone!

Being the youngest child in the family, it seemed to me at the time that everyone else was a little bit insane. But as the years passed, I started to try a bit of heat here and there, and although I still can't say I have my family's superpower to handle the hot stuff, I do love the right chile kick at the right moment. And I find more and more that it's a great way to balance other flavors. This is my version of schug, designed to enjoy the flavor of the fresh cilantro and garlic that I like so much, without the full-on crying effect it can inflict. If you're up to it, feel free to amp up the amount of chiles by as much as you like to cry.

* 2–3 garlic cloves, peeled
* 1–2 green chiles
* 1 large bunch of cilantro (stems and all), roughly chopped
* 1 cup canola or vegetable oil
* 2 tbsp freshly squeezed lemon juice
* 1 tsp Hawaij Spice Mix (see p.20) (or use toasted and ground cumin seeds instead)
* salt, to taste

1. Put the garlic and chiles in a blender or food processor and blend until well combined. Add the cilantro and pulse — we don't want to lose that vibrant green color.

2. Add ¾ cup of the oil, the lemon juice, Hawaij Spice Mix (or cumin) and salt to taste, and pulse — we don't want it to emulsify.

3. Transfer to a sterilized airtight container or jar (see p.24) and top up with the rest of the oil, which will keep it nice and green and help the schug to last longer. It can be kept in the fridge for up to a week.

Tapenade

Makes about 1 cup

* 1 cup pitted Kalamata olives
* leaves from 1 sprig of thyme
* 1 tsp soy sauce
* 1 tbsp olive oil
* 1 tbsp canola or vegetable oil, plus extra for covering

This is a simple yet very useful olive paste that you can use for salad dressings, sandwiches, pasta and fish sauces, or just serve with some good bread. The recipe usually contains anchovies, but I've found that a touch of soy delivers the right level of saltiness while keeping it entirely vegetarian. Feel free, however, to swap the soy for an anchovy fillet.

1. Put all the ingredients except the oils in a blender and blend until well combined. Then while continuing to blend, add the oils gradually.
2. Transfer to a sterilized 1-cup airtight container (see p.24) and add more oil to cover. It can be kept in the fridge for up to 2 weeks. Make sure whenever you use it that you cover it with some extra oil, as this will help the tapenade to stay fresh and last longer.

OUR BACKGROUND

by Layo Paskin

One of my favorite moments in the restaurant is toward the end of the evening shift. Everyone is in, you feel the buzz of both the restaurant and the kitchen bar, and the staff are gliding between customers with ease. Not so long ago, at this time of night, I'd be gearing up to hit the decks at a club in one city or another. So how did I get here?

Zoe and Layo on Hampstead Heath, 1978

I grew up in the heart of London in a close family — all of whom worked in creative fields and all of whom cook, each with their own area of expertise. With my convoluted family history, food and travel have always been intertwined — the more to discover the better.

In 1995 I opened The End nightclub in London, and within three years, I opened a bar restaurant next door called AKA. My DJing and production career launched around the same time: I had residencies in Italy, Spain, Brazil, Argentina, Japan, the USA and regular guest spots pretty much everywhere else. As a DJ you have access to an amazing insider's guide to the places you land, and if it's what you love, it's unmatched. All this time away meant that the business in London needed someone to take over. Enter my younger sister, Zoe.

It feels as though Zoe and I have been working together all our lives. I remember helping our dad and uncle with their hamburger stall in Hampstead, when it still had a market. She was cashier aged four. Zoe returned from running a bar in Barcelona and immediately revolutionized The End and AKA: she ran both places for ten years until we sold. We closed the doors on January 24, 2009. So what next?

In 2012 I was DJing in Israel — Zoe joined me so that we could use the time together to start planning our restaurant idea. A good friend Omri took us to eat at Machneyuda, the incredibly popular restaurant at the heart of the Jerusalem market. It was our third visit, and while there Omri introduced us to Yossi "Papi" Elad. We talked food, we talked restaurants, we talked London… Yossi visited a week later, then came Assaf with a young chef called Tomer. Initially we had talked about a pop-up, but pretty soon we all realized it was meant to be more. Over a handshake in Shoreditch House we decided to open a restaurant. As Zoe says, it started as an arranged marriage but it became a love affair.

Tzatziki

Makes 2¼ cups

In one word: refreshing! In two words: yogurt and cucumbers. Thank god (or maybe the gods?) for the Greeks for giving us this splendid mezze. It's so easy to make and I don't think there's anything you can't have it with — fish, lamb, chicken, you name it. Try to get hold of those cute Dutch cucumbers, as they are packed with flavor. This version is a bit thicker than most tzatzikis because I use labneh with the yogurt, but if you prefer you can simply loosen it with more yogurt to create a chilled yogurt and cucumber soup.

1. Cut the cucumber in half lengthwise and seed it with a spoon, then slice thinly.

2. Place in a mixing bowl with everything but the labneh, yogurt, salt and purslane and mix well.

3. Now add the labneh and yogurt, mix together and season to taste with salt.

4. The tzatziki can be kept in the fridge, in a sterilized airtight container (see p.24), for up to 4 days. To serve, garnish with purslane leaves (if using) and a drizzle of olive oil.

* 1 baby Dutch cucumber, or ½ regular cucumber
* 1 garlic clove, finely grated
* handful of chopped mint leaves
* small handful of chopped parsley
* 2 tbsp freshly squeezed lemon juice
* 1½ tbsp extra virgin olive oil, plus extra to serve
* ½ tsp toasted and ground coriander seeds
* 3 tbsp Labneh (see p.41)
* 1½ cups Greek yogurt
* salt, to taste
* handful of purslane leaves, to garnish (optional)

* 2½ cups Greek yogurt
* 2½ cups natural low-fat yogurt

To serve

* 1 tsp Za'atar Spice Mix (see p.20)
* generous drizzle of extra virgin olive oil

Homemade labneh with za'atar

Makes 2¼ cups

This sour creamy cheese is so easy to make and the taste is ten times better than any ready-made labneh out there. You can find versions of it throughout the Levant and using different kinds of milk — from goats, sheep and cows. My personal favorite is made with cows' milk, as it's less intense in flavor than the other options and has a bright sourness to it. In the restaurant we use this for so many dishes and recipes, but my favorite is simply served with a bit of extra virgin olive oil, some Za'atar and fresh Pita (see p.229) or other bread (I'm a sucker for carbs).

1. Place a double-layered 16-inch square of muslin over a sieve, spoon the yogurts into the middle, then bring the sides together and tie so that you have a nice bundle.
2. Make some space in the fridge and hang your bundle overnight with a small bowl underneath to collect the liquids. Your other option is to hang it outside somewhere (my mama used to hang it over the kitchen sink). Personally I prefer the fridge option, as I like to ensure that the cheese is perfectly chilled. Check it after 5–6 hours — you're looking for it to have stopped dripping.
3. The labneh can be kept in the fridge in a sterilized airtight container (see p.24) for up to 5 days. To serve, spoon into a bowl, make a nice well in the middle, season with the Za'atar Spice Mix and drizzle with olive oil. Grab some bread and…

Spiced olives with rose petals & balsamic vinegar

Makes 2 cups

This very simple spiced olive recipe is packed with flavor. You can serve these as a mezze or for your guests to nibble on at a drinks party. My wife's favorite way to enjoy these is in front of the TV, when she can get through a whole jar without noticing (I've caught her in the act), while mine is to accompany a nice glass of arak with mint and ice.

* ¾ cup Botija olives (if you can't get these plump purple Peruvian olives, use fat Kalamata)
* ¾ cup Moroccan oil-cured black olives (Douce or, if you can't get them, any oil-cured black olives)
* handful of dried rose petals
* ½ tsp crushed red pepper flakes
* 1 tbsp toasted coriander seeds
* ⅔ cup olive oil
* 3 tbsp good-quality balsamic vinegar (no need for the aged stuff, just a good one)
* 4 bay leaves

1. Mix all the ingredients together in a bowl.

2. Transfer to a sterilized 2-cup airtight container or jar (see p.24). Make sure these bad boys are always covered with oil if you're storing them in the cool but not in the fridge (Yaeli, for example, doesn't like hers fridge-cold), where they'll keep for a month. Alternatively, they'll keep in the fridge for 2–3 months.

- ⅔ cup canola oil
- 2 large onions, sliced
- About 1lb trimmed chicken livers
- 2 hard-boiled eggs, peeled and grated
- salt and pepper

To serve

- Challah, toasted (see p.238)
- Chrain (see p.33)
- pickles
- Dijon mustard
- salt and pepper

Hand-chopped chicken liver

Makes about 1 pound

I'm not the biggest fan of chicken liver (maybe due to a childhood overcooked liver trauma, who knows), but one recipe made me a convert and it's this one. The balance of the caramelized onions with the black pepper makes this a winner. We serve this Ashkenazi special gloriously spread on toasted Challah with Chrain, pickles, salt, pepper and Dijon mustard. I use canola oil, but for all you brave souls out there you can go for the full-fat fat version and replace it with chicken or duck fat.

1. Heat a shallow, heavy-bottomed pan over a medium-low heat and add the oil followed by the onions, stirring to coat. You now want to take the time to cook the onions slowly so that they gradually caramelize and turn sweet and light brown in color; this will take around 30–35 minutes, stirring occasionally.

2. Add the livers, turn the heat up to medium and cook for 9–12 minutes — we want them to be cooked all the way through but not to dry them out.

3. Strain and keep the oil in an airtight container for later, then leave the livers and onions to cool before refrigerating. Chilling will help you to chop the livers without making a mess.

4. Once chilled, chop the livers and onions finely and place in a bowl.

5. Add the strained oil, the grated hard-boiled eggs, salt to taste and a generous amount of black pepper, then mix well.

6. The chicken liver can be kept in a sterilized airtight container (see p.24) in the fridge for up to a week. Serve the chicken liver with toasted Challah, Chrain, pickles, and with Dijon mustard and salt and pepper to taste.

Garlic confit cloves & paste

Makes 2¼ cups

So easy to make yet perhaps one of the most versatile ingredients to have in the fridge, Garlic Confit goes into my sauces, stews and pastas. I also add it to vinaigrettes, use it as a sandwich spread or just serve with some nice bread. The low and slow confit cooking makes the garlic sweet and tender or, as my mama calls it, "garlic candy"!

* 6 garlic bulbs, cloves separated and peeled
* 1¼ cups olive oil
* 2 sprigs of thyme

1. You can go one of 2 ways here:

Option 1 Put all the ingredients in a small saucepan over a very, very low heat on the burner. You need to make sure that the oil doesn't start to simmer, otherwise the garlic will burn and turn bitter, and we don't want that. Small, slow bubbles is what we're looking for. From the minute you start seeing small bubbles appear, it should take 30 minutes to cook.

Option 2 Put all the ingredients in an ovenproof dish and roast in a preheated oven at 250°F for 45 minutes.

2. To make garlic confit paste, simply blend in a blender with a bit of the oil.

3. Transfer the cooled cloves and oil or paste to a sterilized airtight container or jar (see p.24). Make sure the paste is always covered with oil, too, and as Papi always says, "Never use your fingers to take it out!" It can be kept in the fridge for 2 weeks.

Baba ganoush

Makes 2¼ cups

We use a very smooth version of this super-famous mezze for the Octo-hummus dish that we serve at the restaurant (see p.138), but it's also great as a standalone mezze, hot or cold. I wanted to create a light hummus here, something you can eat with seafood, so I've replaced the usual chickpeas with charred eggplant. For maximum flavor, make sure you char the eggplant on an open flame, either one by one on the burner or over the hot coals of a barbecue — it's worth the extra effort. In Turkish, this literally translates as "pamper daddy"!

* 4 eggplant
* ¼ cup tahini paste
* 2 tbsp freshly squeezed lemon juice
* drizzle of olive oil
* salt, to taste

1. Prick the eggplant in several places with the tip of a sharp knife so that they won't explode in your face and make a mess in the kitchen. Char the skin of the eggplant on all sides over an open flame on the burner or hot charcoal on a barbecue, turning every 5–6 minutes — the skin needs to harden up and get a bit crispy. There is a third option: set your grill to the highest setting and roast the eggplant in the closest position to the heat source, turning in the same way.

2. Leave the eggplant until cool enough to handle, then peel.

3. Put the eggplant flesh into a blender along with the rest of the ingredients and blend for a good 7–10 minutes — you want the mixture to be very smooth. This can be kept in the fridge, in a sterilized airtight container (see p.24), for up to 4 days.

* 5 tbsp canola oil
* 3 red peppers, cored, seeded and cut into ¾-inch square pieces
* 3 Romano peppers (the pointy red ones — if you can't find them, you can use an additional 3 regular ones), cored, seeded and cut into ¾-inch square pieces
* salt
* 1–2 red chiles, finely chopped (depending on how hot you like it)
* 3–4 garlic cloves, finely sliced
* ½ tsp toasted and ground cumin seeds
* 14.5oz can good-quality chopped tomatoes, strained
* 1 tsp sweet paprika
* Challah, to serve (see p.238)

Matbucha

Makes 3½ cups

One of the biggest stars of Friday night dinner in my house is definitely the Matbucha. My mama makes this tomato and pepper mezze especially for Friday, and by 5pm (after 2–3 hours of cooking) the whole house is filled with an intoxicating peppery-garlicky smell. I wait until my mama is off-guard and sneak a preview with a piece of Challah (see p.238). She uses fresh tomatoes, but in this recipe I've swapped them for canned. It works just as well and saves an hour of cooking.

———

1. The secret of success for this mezze is to keep it on a gentle simmer. Heat a large skillet (the heavier the better) over a medium-low heat. Add the oil, peppers and a pinch of salt, and let them sweat until they collapse. This should take about 35–40 minutes.

2. Add the chiles and cook for 10 minutes, then add the garlic and cumin and cook, stirring, for 2 minutes. At this point your kitchen should be filled with a garlicky aroma, but we're not there yet, so don't dip your Challah! Add the tomatoes and gently simmer for about 30 minutes. The color should become darker and the aroma more intense.

3. This is the time to add the paprika and salt to taste. Simmer for another 10 minutes and adjust the seasoning if necessary. This is a great base for many of the recipes to follow. You can eat it hot or cold, and it will keep in the fridge, in a sterilized airtight container (see p.24), for up to a week. Now for Challah…

* 2¼ cups canola or vegetable oil, for deep-frying
* 2 eggplant, cut into rounds ¾ inch thick
* salt
* 1 tsp sweet paprika
* pinch of crushed red pepper flakes
* 2–3 garlic cloves, finely grated
* 2 tbsp white wine vinegar
* 1 tbsp freshly squeezed lemon juice
* handful of chopped parsley
* handful of chopped scallion
* ½ cup just-boiled water

Sima's eggplant

Fried & lightly cured
Serves 4

I have learned a lot about cooking from my mama. She makes this dish so well that it felt only right to name it after her. It was always there waiting for me when I came home late at night too lazy to actually cook something, so I would grab some bread and dig in. It's punchy and garlicky, and my favorite way to enjoy it is with some White Tahini Sauce (see p.28).

1. Heat the oil for deep-frying in a deep saucepan to 340–350°F — a good way of gauging the temperature without a thermometer is to add a thin slice of potato once the oil starts to heat up, and when you see bubbles around it and it floats a bit, it's ready. I use this method at home when I deep-fry anything. Deep-fry the eggplant rounds one by one for about 3–4 minutes until golden brown, then remove and leave to drain on a tray lined with paper towels. Season with salt.

2. In a bowl, mix all the remaining ingredients together except the parsley and scallion with a pinch of salt and the water added.

3. Arrange the eggplant rounds in layers in a dish, sprinkling each layer as you go with the parsley and scallion.

4. Pour the hot water and spice mixture on top and leave to cool.

5. Cover the dish with plastic wrap and let it rest in the fridge for at least 6 hours, or overnight (I like to give it at least a night). The eggplant can be kept in the fridge, in a sterilized airtight container (see p.24), for up to a week.

Carrot & fennel with harissa & cured lemon

Serves 4

This is a take on a traditional tangy carrot salad that you'll find on almost any table (well, any Moroccan table) at Friday night dinner. It's sour and spicy, just how I love it. And to make it a bit fresher than the original version I grew up with, I've added some fresh fennel and toasted coriander seeds. It goes brilliantly as a side with grilled fish or seafood, and I also like it with cold meat cuts.

———

1. Boil the carrots in plenty of salted water for 5 minutes (they still need to be a bit firm), then drain and leave to cool to room temperature.

2. Place the carrots with the rest of the ingredients in a bowl and mix together, then leave to rest for 20 minutes before serving. This dish can be kept in the fridge, in a sterilized airtight container (see p.24), for up to 4 days.

* 3 carrots, peeled and cut into rounds ¼ inch thick
* salt
* 1 fennel bulb, sliced (if the outer layer is tough, discard it)
* handful of chopped parsley
* handful of chopped cilantro
* 1½ tbsp Harissa (see p.27) (you can go for 2 if you like it spicy)
* 1 tbsp Cured Lemon Paste (see p.25)
* 1 tsp toasted and ground coriander seeds
* 1 tsp toasted and ground cumin seeds
* ¼ cup freshly squeezed lemon juice
* 2 tbsp rice vinegar
* ¼ cup canola oil
* drizzle of olive oil

- * 1 cup dried white beans, soaked in 2½ cups cold water overnight
- * 14 cups water
- * 1 tbsp fennel seeds in a muslin sachet (optional)
- * ½ red onion, chopped
- * 2 scallions (green and white parts), chopped
- * handful of chopped parsley
- * handful of chopped mint
- * 1 tsp toasted and ground cumin seeds
- * 5 tbsp olive oil, plus an extra drizzle to garnish
- * 3 tbsp freshly squeezed lemon juice
- * ½ tsp sugar
- * salt and pepper, to taste
- * ⅔ cup Velvet Tomatoes (see p.30)
- * 2 hard-boiled eggs, peeled
- * Maldon salt flakes, to garnish

A take on piyaz

Serves 4

When I first made this bean salad for the restaurant, I thought I'd invented a new killer bean salad. It was only after I did some research for this book that I found out that the Turks know a lot more about beans than me. They have a very similar version of this salad, using cooked beans, coursely chopped tomatoes, hard-boiled egg quarters and loads of sliced onion. The tomatoes and the egg are great friends to the bean, and by using the Velvet Tomatoes you get a fun play of textures.

———

1. Drain the soaked beans and place them in a large pan with the sachet of fennel seeds (if using — this gives the beans a great flavor), cover with the 14 cups water and bring to a boil. Then reduce the heat and simmer for 2–3 hours, skimming off the foam from time to time. The beans should be soft but not falling apart. (If cooking them in a pressure cooker, they will need an hour.)

2. Drain the cooked beans and leave them to cool. Place in a mixing bowl and mix with the onions, herbs and cumin. Then dress with the olive oil and lemon juice, and season with the sugar and salt and pepper to taste.

3. To serve, divide the Velvet Tomatoes among 4 plates (or one large platter) and then spoon over the bean salad, grate over the boiled eggs, drizzle with extra olive oil and sprinkle with pepper and Maldon salt flakes.

——— *Afiyet olsun!*
(Bon appétit in Turkish)

Chickpeas with spinach & yogurt

Serves 6

I love the combination of hot and cold in salads, and legumes make the ideal candidates for either role. I really like the extra kick that you get from chiles, and the fresh lemon cubes. Feel free to use this trick every time you are looking for extra zestiness in a salad. This combination works excellently.

1. Drain and wash the chickpeas, place in a saucepan and cover with the 10 cups water. Bring to a boil, then reduce the heat and simmer for an hour, skimming off the foam from time to time. The chickpeas should be tender but not mushy — cook for a little longer if necessary.

2. Meanwhile, prep all the vegetables and herbs and place in a large bowl.

3. Once the chickpeas are done, drain and add to the bowl. Then add the oil and lemon juice, season to taste with salt and pepper and mix gently.

4. Divide the yogurt among 6 plates (or go for one big one) and top with the salad. Drizzle with more extra virgin olive oil and enjoy.

* 1 cup dried chickpeas (the small Bulgarian kind are my favorite choice here), soaked overnight in 8½ cups cold water
* 10 cups cold water
* 1 large tomato, cut into ¾-inch cubes
* 1 bunch of spinach, washed, trimmed and roughly chopped, about 6 cups
* 1 small unwaxed lemon, first sliced into rounds ½ inch thick, then seeded and cut into ½-inch cubes, including the rind
* 1 green chile, seeded and diced
* handful of chopped parsley
* handful of chopped mint
* 2 garlic cloves, finely grated (a Microplane grater is the best for this job)
* 5 tbsp extra virgin olive oil, plus a nice drizzle at the end
* 2½ tbsp freshly squeezed lemon juice
* salt and pepper, to taste
* 6 tbsp Greek yogurt

* 2 butternut squashes, about 2¾ lbs in total, peeled, seeded and cut into smallish chunks
* 1¾ cups water
* ¼ cup olive oil, plus an extra drizzle to garnish
* 1–2 tbsp Harissa (see p.27) (depending on how hot you like it; I like it pretty hot)
* 2 tbsp Cured Lemon Paste (see p.25)
* 5 Garlic Confit Cloves (see p.46), optional
* 1 tsp toasted and ground cumin seeds
* 1 tsp toasted and ground coriander seeds
* 1 tsp sweet paprika
* ½ tsp toasted and ground caraway seeds (optional)
* squeeze of lemon juice
* salt, to taste
* ½ cup Greek yogurt, to serve
* chopped parsley, to garnish

Tirshi

Tunisian butternut squash mezze

Makes 2¼ cups

This Tunisian mezze is super-easy to make and packed with flavor. I also like to use it with meat and offal dishes (see the recipe for lambs' tongues on p.178), but it works equally well as a side for couscous or even grilled fish and seafood. As a mezze, I prefer to serve it warmish with a little yogurt, but it's good cold, too.

1. Place the butternut squash in a small pan, add the 1¾ cups water and bring to a boil, then simmer vigorously until the water has evaporated.

2. Add the oil and reduce the heat to minimum — we want the squash to slowly dry out, and as you stir it occasionally with a fork, it needs to fall apart into nice strings, which should take around 40–50 minutes.

3. Once the squash is dry, add the rest of the ingredients except the yogurt and parsley and mix in with a fork until all is absorbed and tasty.

4. Wait for it to cool slightly, then serve over a layer of Greek yogurt and scatter with chopped parsley and drizzle with olive oil to finish.

Burned eggplant with tahini & pomegranate

Serves 4 as a mezze

You can think of this as a deconstructed Baba Ganoush (see p.51). To get the maximum flavor from the eggplant it's best to char them over an open flame on the burner or on a charcoal barbecue.

* 2 eggplant, charred over an open flame and peeled (see p.51)
* salt and pepper, to taste
* juice of ½ lemon
* 4 tbsp extra virgin olive oil, plus an extra drizzle to garnish

For the garnish

* 4 tbsp White Tahini Sauce (see p.28)
* 4 tbsp pomegranate seeds
* handful of chopped fresh cilantro

1. Arrange the whole burned eggplant on a serving plate, then season to taste with salt and pepper and dress with the lemon juice and olive oil.

2. Drizzle the White Tahini Sauce on top, sprinkle with the pomegranate seeds and the chopped cilantro and drizzle with a little more olive oil. You can keep the peeled eggplant in an airtight container in the fridge for up to 2–3 days and then, when you want to serve, simply heat them up and add your garnishes.

- 2½ cups dried chickpeas, soaked in 12½ cups cold water overnight
- about 3–4 tbsp flour (I like to use chickpea/gram flour)
- 1 tsp salt
- ½ tsp toasted and ground cumin seeds
- 1¾ pints canola oil, for deep-frying
- White Tahini Sauce, to serve (see p.28)

Falafel

by Yossi Elad

Makes around 30 small balls

Falafel is one of the most common street foods in Israel. It can be made from lentils, white beans or dried fava (broad) beans, but in Israel we make it from chickpeas. I learned how to make falafel from the Iraqi grandmother of a friend of mine. The best way to learn is to watch: the movement of the hands, the quantities of ingredients… These are things that our grandmothers can't explain in words — they usually just say, "Put in as much as it takes" or "…as much as it needs."

1. Drain the chickpeas and mince them, ideally in a meat grinder using the largest holes (such as the one that comes with your electric mixer).

2. Add the flour, salt and cumin to the chickpeas — don't be tempted to add too much flour, as that will make your falafel hard and dense.

3. Using wet hands, roll the mixture into balls a bit smaller than Ping-Pong balls.

4. Heat the oil for deep-frying in a deep saucepan to 340–350°F (if you haven't got a thermometer see p.55). Deep-fry the balls, in batches, for 4–5 minutes until well browned, then remove and drain on a tray lined with paper towels.

5. Serve the falafel hot with White Tahini Sauce.

Variations

In the restaurant, I make what we call fish falafel by adding a mixed bunch of parsley and cilantro and about ½lb mixed skinless fish fillets and shellfish to the mixture. Just add the additional ingredients to the mincer with the chickpeas and mince together, then roll into balls and deep-fry as above. Feel free to experiment with different legumes and herbs as well, and other spices.

WINE
by Layo Paskin

_____ No matter where wine was first made, there is no doubt that the Middle East is the birthplace of the culture of drinking wine. Hugh Johnson & Jancis Robinson

The earliest wine manifestos were written by the Phoenicians, based in Canaan (Lebanon). They planned vineyards according to climate and topography, extending their influence and culture through the very heart of what we consider the footprint of our cuisine, from the Levant (Lebanon, Algeria, Tunisia, Egypt, Israel...) to Sicily and Spain. Only recently a cellar was discovered in what would have been their land in northern Israel, dating from 3700BC. With the advent of Islam, drinking wine was forbidden to Muslims, but Jews in the Middle East were able to lease land for wine cultivation. Advances in mathematics and alchemy led to the understanding of distilling, and even the very word "alcohol" (al-koh'l) is derived from the Arabic.

Over time, regional wine-making and culinary traditions have evolved together, and many local cuisines are naturally paired with local wines. This is what we echo at The Palomar, where we have created a wine list that complements the ingredients used in our food. We look for the new and unexplored, small, independent producers. Some of the wines will have had minimal human intervention, some will be organic and biodynamic, and generally all are unusual wines with a story. We do love a story.

We change our rolling wine list seasonally, we spend a long time with suppliers finding wines that are rarer and producers who are passionate about their wine. Luckily, many are not driven by profit, but by love. (As the old adage goes, to make a small fortune in wine, start with a large one!)

With regard to red wines, we love the spice of Syrah, the smoothness of Pinot Noir, the body of a Nero d'Avola (Arabic influence) and the deep berry flavors of a Cabernet Sauvignon. As for white wines, we enjoy the richness of a Chardonnay in all its myriad forms, dry Rieslings and Albariño. But the list just goes on... With even the slight promise of sun, rosé combines with our food flavors perfectly.

————

Clos De Gat winery, 1958. Photograph © Yoav Alon

Beet carpaccio with a lentil tuile

See p.70–1

Beet carpaccio with a lentil tuile

Serves 6

This dish is the result of a collaboration between me and my sous chef Mitz. He came up with the lentil tuile, which unwittingly references an Arab dish (originally from Iraq) called mujadarah *(meaning "pockmark"): a stew of rice and lentils with lots of caramelized onions. Working on this dish was a lot of fun — the testing, tasting and then the massive satisfaction with the end result. The tuile takes a bit of preparation, but it makes a great nibble. They keep well for a week easily, so go the extra mile and bake a double batch if you can.*

If you're going for the full tuile experience, begin a day in advance; if not, start with the beet, and while they're cooking, prep the rest.

1. To make the lentil tuile, put all the ingredients except the oil and salt in a saucepan and bring to a boil, then reduce the heat and simmer gently for about an hour until very soft; the lentils and rice should be really overcooked and mushy. If at some point you feel it needs a bit more water, then add it so that it doesn't burn.

2. Blitz the lentil mixture in a food processor or blender or with an immersion blender, then turn out on to a baking sheet lined with a silicone mat (ordinary parchment paper will absorb the moisture and the mixture will stick to it) and spread with a metal spatula as thinly as possible. Let dry overnight at room temperature. Alternatively, place in your oven on its lowest setting to use it as a dehydrator and leave for 3–4 hours to dry out, checking on it every hour or so.

3. Heat the oil for deep-frying in a deep saucepan to 340–350°F (see p.55). Meanwhile, break the dried lentil sheet into 2-inch squares. Deep-fry the tuile, in batches, for about a minute until lightly browned. Gently remove to a tray lined with paper towels to absorb the oil and season with salt straight away — this will help the tuile to crisp up fast and make sure they won't be too oily, as the end result should be light and crispy.

4. To make the beet carpaccio, preheat your oven to 350°F. Rub the beets with 2 tablespoons of the olive oil and wrap each of them individually in foil — baking them in their skins and the foil will ensure that the beets cook perfectly and that the flavor is intense and bright. Place on a baking sheet and bake for 1 hour. To check that they're cooked through, pierce with a knife — if it slides in easily, they're done, but if not, give them an extra 10–30 minutes (some beets are gigantic).

5. Once cooked, remove the beets from the oven and set aside to cool. Then put on some gloves (it's gonna get a bit messy), peel the foil off — the skin will come off easily with it — then slice ⅛ inch thick. A mandoline really comes in handy in these situations

For the lentil tuile
* 2½ tbsp dried Puy lentils
* 2½ tbsp sushi rice
* 1¾ cups water
* 1 tsp toasted and ground cumin seeds
* 4½ cups canola oil, for deep-frying
* salt, to taste

For the beet carpaccio
* 3 large beets, skin on, washed and patted dry
* ½ cup olive oil
* Maldon salt flakes and freshly ground black pepper
* 3 tbsp toasted and chopped hazelnuts (see p.21)
* 3 tbsp pomegranate seeds
* ½ cup goats' cheese
* handful of micro basil (or use finely chopped regular basil if you can't get hold of this)
* handful of micro sorrel (ditto)

For the horseradish yogurt

* 5 tbsp Greek yogurt
* 1 tsp Chrain (see p.33) or finely grated horseradish
* finely grated zest of ¼ unwaxed lemon
* salt, to taste
* finely chopped hazelnuts, toasted, to garnish (see p.21, optional)

For the dressing

* 4 tbsp pomegranate molasses
* 3 tbsp date syrup
* 1 tsp freshly squeezed lemon juice
* 1 tbsp balsamic vinegar
* salt, to taste

and they are inexpensive, so get one! But watch your fingertips, as you'll be needing them later. Set aside until you're ready with all the other elements.

6. For both the horseradish yogurt and the dressing, mix together each set of ingredients in separate mixing bowls and season to taste with salt.

7. If you have some plastic squeezy bottles, decant the horseradish yogurt and the dressing into 2 separate bottles. These bottles are cheap to buy and are great for adding sauces and dressings to a finished dish.

8. To serve, divide the beet slices between serving plates, arranging them in a single layer with minimal overlapping, then season to taste with salt and pepper. Add the dressing, drizzle over the remaining olive oil and sprinkle with the hazelnuts and pomegranate seeds.

9. On a baking sheet, break the goats' cheese into 25–30 chunks and scorch with a blowtorch. If you don't have a blowtorch, a good way to do this is to preheat your grill to its highest setting and place the tray in the closest position to the heat source for about a minute.

10. To serve, divide the cheese between the plates. Add the horseradish yogurt in small dollops to each plate and sprinkle over some finely chopped, toasted hazelnuts if you like. If you've gone for the tuile, add 5–6 small pieces to each plate. Lastly, garnish with the micro herbs. Nothing can beat this!

Papi's pickled okra

by Yossi Elad

Makes 4 cups

Okra was not a vegetable we ate in my family, so the first time I tasted it was when I moved to Jerusalem. The Azura restaurant in the Machane Yehuda market used to serve okra cooked with tomatoes, and while the dish smelled great I didn't like the look of it. I sampled the green "ladies' fingers" (as some people call okra) raw and realized that they aren't actually very tasty, which made me determined to find a way to work with this vegetable to which I was a stranger. I wanted my okra to be really appetizing, so I decided to try pickling them. I went on to research and develop more recipes for pickled okra, but this is my very first one, which I still make to this day.

* About 1lb okra, washed and air-dried
* 1 unwaxed lemon, sliced
* 2 whole chiles
* 1 small bunch of dill
* 5 garlic cloves, peeled
* 3¼ cups water
* 2½ tbsp coarse sea salt
* 1 tsp sugar

1. Arrange the okra in a sterilized 2⅓-cup airtight jar (see p.24) standing upright in a neat circle. Tuck the lemon slices, chiles, dill and garlic cloves in between the okra.

2. Pour the 3¼ cups water into a saucepan over a medium heat and stir in the salt until it has dissolved. Add the sugar and bring to a boil, then pour the hot liquid into the jar, covering the okra.

3. Seal the jar and leave it to do its pickling thing for 3–4 days in a cool, dark place. They will keep for up to 3–4 weeks.

Variations

Black peppercorns or other spices can be added to the jar. If you want to pickle baby cucumbers instead, omit the lemon and skip bringing the brine to the boil, but you will need to add 1 tablespoon white wine vinegar or cider vinegar.

Zucchini machluta with tulum cheese

Makes 2¼ cups

In "hummus speak" (I swear there is such a language), the word machluta *is used to describe a chunky cooked chickpea and fava (broad) bean topping added to the hummus — it's a bit like Masabacha (hummus with whole chickpeas) yet totally different. The meaning of the Arabic word* machluta *is "gravel road," probably alluding to the dish's gravelly texture. You know how it is with food and culture: every group has a different interpretation of it. In my house,* machluta *is a zucchini mezze that you whip up when you've made stuffed zucchinis* (kussa mahchi) *and you don't want to throw away the insides of the vegetable (we never waste anything in the kitchen). I guess it shares the name because of its chunky texture. I like to serve it with tulum cheese — a great Turkish cheese, but if you can't find it just use feta — which works really well with the acidity of the machluta. You can also use it for sandwiches, pastas, on rice or whatever you feel like, and it works either cold, hot or at room temperature.*

* ¼ cup olive oil, plus extra to serve
* 1 large white onion, chopped
* salt and pepper, to taste
* 3 garlic cloves, finely chopped
* 6 zucchinis, grated (I like to use the white Italian ones, but regular green ones will do just fine)
* 1 tsp Hawaij Spice Mix (see p.20) (can be replaced with ½ tsp toasted and ground cumin and ¼ tsp ground turmeric)
* ¼ tsp ground turmeric
* 3 tbsp freshly squeezed lemon juice

To serve

* 1 tbsp chopped parsley
* 3–4 tbsp tulum (or feta) cheese

1. Heat a wide saucepan over a medium heat, add the oil and the onion along with some salt and pepper and sauté for 5–7 minutes until golden. Add the garlic and cook, stirring, for 2 minutes.

2. Add the zucchinis, crank up the heat a bit and cook for 20 minutes, stirring every 5 minutes or so, as we want to extract all the liquid from the zucchinis and concentrate the flavor to the max.

3. Stir in the Hawaij Spice Mix and turmeric and cook for another 15 minutes over a medium heat. Keep stirring — we don't want it sticking to the base of the pan.

4. By now the juices should have concentrated and the zucchini "hummus" dried out nicely to a chunky consistency. If not, then continue to cook a bit more (it all depends on the water content of the zucchinis, which varies with the type, size and time of year). Once you're there, it's time to season with salt, pepper and the lemon juice. Take off the heat and serve, or leave to cool or eat straight from the pan.

5. To serve, sprinkle with the parsley, the cheese and some extra olive oil. The Machluta can be kept in a sterilized airtight container (see p.24) in the fridge for up to 5 days.

* 6⅓ cups canola oil, for deep-frying
* 2 sweet potatoes, peeled and then shaved with a peeler
* 1½ tbsp Jerusalem Spice Mix (see p.18)
* salt, to taste
* 4–5 tbsp Greek yogurt, to serve
* 2 tbsp Schug (see p.34), to garnish

Sweet potato fries with yogurt & Schug

Makes a 8 – 12-cup boxful

This is easily the most addictive snack we serve at the restaurant. Sometimes a good nishnoosh ("nibble" in Hebrew) goes a long way, especially with a good movie and some beer or as a snack with a side for dipping. We serve it with yogurt and Schug, but any other dip will do the trick — Harissa Aïoli (see p.92), soured cream or a salsa. You can fry them up to 3–4 days in advance, and if they're fried, dried and stored properly in an airtight container, they can last even longer. This recipe uses sweet potato, but you can easily make it with parsnip or celeriac.

1. Heat the oil for deep-frying in a deep saucepan to 325–340°F — you can test to see if you have the right oil temperature by frying one of the potato shavings, which should take 2–3 minutes to fry.

2. Deep-fry the shavings, in small batches, making sure they cook evenly all over, for 2–3 minutes. Remove to trays lined with paper towels and season generously with the Jerusalem Spice Mix and salt.

3. Make sure you don't pile the fries up but spread them out in a single layer, then leave to dry for at least 15 minutes before you serve or store them. Change the paper towels from time to time during the drying time to make sure all the excess oil is absorbed.

4. Serve the fries with a side of the yogurt, topped with the Schug.

- 2 red peppers
- 2 tomatoes
- 2 green chiles (1 if you're afraid of the heat)
- 2 garlic cloves, very finely chopped
- salt and pepper
- ½ tsp toasted and ground cumin seeds
- ¼ tsp toasted and ground caraway seeds (optional)
- 2 tbsp freshly squeezed lemon juice
- 3 tbsp olive oil

Salata mashwiya

Makes about 1 cup

Mashwiya is a great salad/mezze made from Tunisian spicy chiles, peppers and tomato. Why is it so great? Because it's burned! The meaning of the word mashwiya *in Arabic is literally "roasted in fire." We didn't get a Josper charcoal oven for the restaurant just because it's pretty, but because we love smoky flavors. Now I know this is a bit messy, but it's worth it… Place some foil around your burner or use a barbecue outdoors. We like to season this dish on a chopping board while it's still hot, but you can also wait for it to cool and season it more neatly in a mixing bowl.*

———

1. Char the peppers, tomatoes and chiles on all sides over an open flame on the burner or hot charcoal on a barbecue, turning frequently, until black all over. Place in an airtight container or plastic bag and wait for the ingredients to cool slightly, then peel — this will make the peeling process much easier.

2. Cut the peppers down the middle and discard the seeds and stems. Discard the stems from the chiles, but I don't discard the seeds, as that's where all the heat is. However, feel free to do so if you want a mellower result.

3. Cut the tomatoes into chunks, place on a large chopping board with the peppers, chiles and garlic and chop together.

4. Season with salt and pepper to taste, the spices, lemon juice and olive oil, "chopping" them in, too.

5. Transfer to your serving dish, or a sterilized airtight container (see p.24) if storing. Then — this is the most important bit — mop the board with a piece of bread and enjoy. This can be served hot, cold or at room temperature, and kept in the fridge for up to 5 days.

Mkhallal

Pickled turnip & beet

Makes 6⅓ cups

As a child I knew winter was coming when my father made this dish. I have a very vivid memory of huge pickling jars sitting on the kitchen counter filled with turnips and beets. I remember it looked like magic to me as my father stacked up these white and purple vegetables together in the jars and after a week they emerged all purple and pinkish. When they were ready he was always happy, and made sure that everyone within a five-mile radius tasted them to check that they were satisfied with the result as well. Every time I go back home to visit and I see a big purple jar, I feel like a child again because then I can be sure of two things: my father will soon be in a good mood, and winter is coming.

* 2¼ lbs peeled and trimmed turnips, cut into ¾-inch wedges, about 3–5 turnips
* 2 beets, peeled, trimmed and cut into ¾-inch wedges
* 1 small green chile, sliced
* 2 dried bay leaves (optional)
* 1 garlic clove, sliced
* 2¼ cups just-boiled water
* ⅔ cup distilled vinegar
* 2 tbsp kosher salt
* 1 tsp sugar

1. In a sterilized 6½-cup jar (see p.24), arrange the turnips, beets, chile, bay leaves (if using) and garlic.

2. Mix the rest of the ingredients together until the salt and sugar have dissolved.

3. Pour the liquid into the jar, making sure all ingredients are properly covered, let cool and then seal.

4. Leave in a place with sunlight for a week (a kitchen counter is great), then transfer to the fridge. They can be kept in the fridge for 2 months.

As always, don't use your fingers to take the pickles out of the jar.

RAW
BEGINNINGS

―――――

I think it's pretty obvious what this chapter is about: raw everything — fish, seafood, vegetables. What a great way to start a meal, with food that is fresh, clean, healthy and natural. But I chose the title for this chapter also because it reflects my own beginnings in cooking.

I grew up in a fairly traditional Jewish home, with no shellfish, no raw fish and, for sure, no bacon. As far back as I can recall, I was curious about tasting anything new and different. I still remember the first time I tasted mussels: I was 16 and my big brother Amir took me to the Jerusalem restaurant Adom (which, funnily enough, was the first restaurant at which The Palomar's Assaf Granit worked as head chef). I had mussels with tomatoes and vodka, and I was hooked there and then. The first sashimi I ever ate was Uri Navon's famous yellowtail with strawberries, wasabi and pickled diakon at his restaurant in Israel — it was mind-blowing!

When I started working with raw ingredients as a young cook, everything was new and exciting, and I fell in love with the textures, flavors and prepping techniques. Filleting my first fish by myself (to this day it's my favorite prep), cleaning my first batch of shrimp, shucking my first oyster — the surprises never stopped. One day it was a Japanese approach, the next it was Spanish, and the train kept on going...

The first dishes I created and felt proud of were raw fish and seafood. I couldn't lean on my heritage — I had to do it on my own and push my boundaries. Slowly, something wonderful happened and it all started to come together — the old and the new — into a melting pot of all I've learned.

by Tomer Amedi

Moroccan oysters

Serves 4

The city of Oualidia is where Morocco's oysters come from, though this dish is named not after the place, but the serving style. An homage to the classic Tabasco and vinegar, here we use instead Harissa oil and fresh lemon zest.

* 12 fresh oysters (I like medium-sized rock oysters)
* 1 tbsp Harissa (see p.27)
* 1 unwaxed lemon
* 12 cilantro leaves, to garnish

1. Shuck the oysters, making sure no debris is left in the bottom part of the shells, that the oyster meat is loose and that you haven't allowed the juices to spill out (that's the best bit!).

2. Drizzle a couple of drops of harissa oil onto each oyster. Using a Microplane or any other fine grater, grate a little lemon zest onto each one and then cut the lemon and squeeze a bit of lemon juice on top.

3. Garnish with the cilantro leaves and serve.

* 8–10 fresh scallops, cleaned
* handful of chopped parsley
* handful of chopped cilantro
* handful of chopped mint
* 1 shallot, finely chopped
* handful of toasted cashew nuts, finely chopped
* 1 tbsp dried barberries or chopped dried cranberries
* salt, to taste
* ¼ cup lime juice
* 2½ tbsp canola or vegetable oil
* pinch of sugar
* Maldon salt flakes, to taste

For the garnish

* 1 lime
* ½ green chile, finely sliced
* 2–3 scallions, green parts only, cut into 2-inch pieces and sliced into thin strips — put these right into iced water to retain their vibrancy, and you'll see that they also curl up very prettily to make Curly Scallions
* drizzle of olive oil

Scallop carpaccio with "Thai-bouleh"

Cashew & lime tabbouleh
Serves 4

This is a fantastic dish we made for one of the first tasting menus at the restaurant. It's funny how cuisines you don't normally associate with one another actually feature similar flavor profiles: both Thai and Lebanese cooking share the love of sour and lots of herbs. So as weird as it may sound, it feels pretty natural to play with them both. The traditional bulgur in tabbouleh is replaced here with finely chopped toasted cashews, and the lemon with lime.

1. Slice the scallops into thin discs and arrange them on 4 chilled serving plates.

2. To make the "Thai-bouleh," combine the herbs, shallot, cashews and dried barberries (or cranberries) in a mixing bowl. Season to taste with salt, half the lime juice, the oil and sugar.

3. Season the scallops with Maldon salt flakes and a touch of lime juice, then divide the Thai-bouleh between the plates, making sure that it covers all the scallops — you want to taste it in each bite.

4. Cut off the top and bottom of the lime with a serrated knife. Sit the fruit on the chopping board and cut away the rind and white pith from the top to the bottom, turning the fruit around until only the flesh is left. Cut between the membranes to extract the pristine, pith-free segments.

5. To serve, garnish with the lime segments, sliced chile, Curly Scallions, and a drizzle of olive oil. Serve immediately.

Sashimi Uri style

Serves 4

"This one is for good luck," I said to chef Assaf when we sat down to write our first draft menu. "Can't open a restaurant without this one!" he replied. It worked when we opened Machneyuda, it worked for The Palomar and I think it will work for you with your guests! Chef Uri was the one who came up with this fresh sashimi dish back in 2006 (when we were young and beautiful; OK, maybe just young) and it has remained with us ever since. The tanginess of the cured onion and the pickled ginger vinaigrette is perfect with the richness of a fatty fish, and the cucumber salad refreshes the palate between those two strong tastes.

---

1. To make the cured onions, the day before, bring all the ingredients except the onions to a simmer in a saucepan and cook until the sugar has dissolved.

2. Place the onions in a sterilized airtight container or jar (see p.24), then pour the liquid over the onions, making sure they are fully covered. Let cool and then seal and refrigerate overnight. They will keep in the fridge for up to 2 weeks.

3. To make the pickled ginger vinaigrette, in a blender, blend the pickled ginger and liquid, garlic, date syrup, vinegar, mirin, salt and lemon juice together. Once blended, add the oils slowly, while blending, until emulsified.

4. Slice the cucumber into spaghetti-like strands. The easiest way to do this is with a mandoline, but if you don't have one (although you really should get one, as it will make life so much easier, trust me!), then cut into thin slices lengthwise with a knife and then "spaghetti" them. Place in a mixing bowl and season with salt, the lemon juice and a touch of olive oil.

5. Take the cured onions out of their liquid (remember to use tongs), and remove the core root so that you can separate them into nice segments.

6. Slice the fish last, then start to assemble the dish. Place 5 onion segments on each plate, then the fish on top of each onion segment and garnish each piece with a slice of radish, slice of apple, a cilantro leaf and Maldon salt flakes. Place the cucumber salad on the side of each plate and garnish each sashimi with a slice of chile.

7. The final step you need to do at the table is to drizzle the vinaigrette over each piece of fish, as we want to keep it as fresh as possible.

---

* 1 baby Dutch cucumber — remember, if you can't find one, you can use ½ English (regular) one
* salt, to taste
* 4 tsp freshly squeezed lemon juice
* olive oil, for drizzling
* ⅔ lb loin of fresh hamachi (yellowtail), salmon or line-caught tuna
* 3 French radishes, thinly sliced and soaked in iced water
* 1 Granny Smith apple, quartered, cored and thinly sliced
* 20 cilantro leaves
* Maldon salt flakes, to garnish
* 1 green chile, thinly sliced

For the cured onions

* ¼ cup olive oil
* ¼ cup freshly squeezed lemon juice
* ¼ cup white wine vinegar
* ¼ cup sugar
* 2 small red onions, cut into quarters

For the pickled ginger vinaigrette

* 2 tbsp pickled ginger (with the pickling liquid)
* 1 small garlic clove, peeled
* 1 tbsp date syrup
* 1 tbsp rice vinegar
* 1 tbsp mirin
* pinch of salt
* 4 tsp freshly squeezed lemon juice
* 1 tbsp olive oil, plus extra to season
* 1 tbsp canola or vegetable oil

For the gazpacho

* 5 large good-quality ripe tomatoes, cut into quarters
* ¼ cucumber, peeled and roughly chopped
* ½ red pepper, cored, seeded and roughly chopped
* ½–1 red chile, sliced
* ½ red onion, roughly chopped
* 1 Granny Smith apple, cored and roughly chopped
* ½ thin slice of Challah (see p.238) (or any white fluffy bread), crust removed
* ½ tsp toasted and ground cumin seeds
* ½ tsp Za'atar Spice Mix (see p.20)
* salt, to taste
* handful of basil leaves
* handful of cilantro leaves
* 3 tbsp olive oil
* 2–3 tbsp freshly squeezed lemon juice
* 2–3 tbsp rice vinegar
* 1–3 ice cubes, if needed for thinning

Scallop tartare with Middle Eastern gazpacho

Serves 6

Nothing beats a cold, refreshing gazpacho on a hot summer's day, but I've found it works well with raw fish and seafood dishes any day of the year. For this version, I've swerved a bit from the classic Andalusian recipe, adding herbs, apples and spices, taking it on a journey from Spain to the center of Jerusalem and from there on to London.

Feel free to tweak the recipe. You could, for instance, add some bread to give it more body — ideal if you're serving it on its own. And do play with the herbs and vegetables. Fish such as tuna or salmon can also be substituted for the scallops if you prefer. Go ahead and experiment with different ingredients, spices and flavors.

----

1. To make the gazpacho, place all the vegetables, the apple and the dry ingredients in a blender or food processor and blitz on full speed for 2–3 minutes. Add the herbs and liquids and blitz for another minute. The consistency should be like heavy cream — if it's too thick, you can add the ice cubes to the blender or food processor.

2. Check the mixture for salt, then strain through a fine sieve into a bowl. Cover with plastic wrap and chill in the fridge for at least 2 hours before you serve.

3. For the tartare, combine all the ingredients except the radish in a bowl and check for seasoning.

4. To serve, divide the tartare between serving bowls and garnish with sliced radish. Take the gazpacho out of the fridge and give it a good shake, transfer to a beautiful serving pitcher and pour into each bowl at the table at the last minute.

For the tartare

* 8 large fresh scallops (hand-dived are the best), cleaned and cut into ½-inch cubes
* 1 large tomato, seeded and diced into ¼-inch cubes
* handful of chopped parsley
* 6 black Moroccan olives, pitted and chopped (Greek Thassos olives are also good)
* ½ red onion, finely diced
* 1 slice of Challah (see p.238), crust removed and cut into ½-inch cubes, then dried out in an oven preheated to 275°F for 15 minutes
* 2½ tbsp freshly squeezed lemon juice
* 4 tbsp olive oil
* salt and pepper, to taste
* 1 radish, finely sliced, to garnish

HERITAGE

by Layo Paskin

At The Palomar it's never just business, it's always personal. Each of us has a family history filled with stories, quirks and surprises, tragedies and serendipitous romances.

Zoe and I spent a huge amount of our childhood at our paternal grandmother's house. An only child born to an English publican mother and a Swiss–French father, Nana (Betty) Paskin was a hairdresser in London's West End. Our grandfather, Lewis Paskin, was a poor East End Russian Jew. One of nine children, he was the first to be born in England after the family fled Russia's 1907 pogroms. After losing his hair in an accident at age 11, he always wore a hat. That's also when he started to smoke, and I seldom saw him without that hat or a cigarette. To earn money for the family, he used to ask West End theatergoers at the end of a matinee for their programs. He'd then race home, where a sister would iron the programs, so he could resell them for the evening performance.

Lewis and Betty Paskin, 1958

How did these two very different people meet? At a dance. My grandma noticed him because he was a terrific dancer, though he wasn't the handsome stranger she wished for. He persuaded her that they should just dance together until she met someone she wanted to fall in love with. This story always makes me cry. But as he would always tell me, she did fall in love with him...

Our mother was born to a Polish Jewish woman and an already married Irishman and was adopted by a couple who were Austrian and German refugees. The rest of their families were killed in Auschwitz. I once asked Nana Mimi why she never cried, and she said she had used up all her tears.

Nana Mimi was an amazing baker, bringing European elegance to our plates and palates with goulash, Sachertorte, strudel; while Nana Betty would make a crazy amalgamation of English classics and Ashkenazi hits. Our background, with its emphasis on good food, hospitality, openness and empathy, has influenced not just our palates but our approach to our work and our lives.

Cured mackerel fricassee

Serves 4

Street food is always a good source of inspiration, this being a classic example. Fricassee is a Tunisian savory deep-fried bun, like a doughnut, usually filled with canned tuna, hard-boiled egg, potatoes and harissa (some also include cured lemons, olives or chiles), and it tastes so good. For The Palomar, I wanted to create a version that uses local ingredients and elevates it, while retaining the spirit of the original dish. I recommend curing a larger quantity of mackerel, as it will keep for up to a week in the fridge and it's also great to serve as a mezze or in sandwiches.

1. For the cured mackerel, cut the mackerel fillets into 12 evenly sized pieces. Spread one-third of the Maldon salt over a tray, place the mackerel on top and cover with the rest of the salt. Leave the fish buried in the salt for 25 minutes, then remove from the salt, rinse lightly and pat completely dry with paper towels.

2. Combine the oils in an airtight container. Add the spices and thyme sprig, then the mackerel and leave in the fridge overnight for the fish to absorb the flavors.

3. The next day, make sure you take the mackerel out using a clean and dry pair of tongs!

4. For the new potatoes, boil the potatoes in a pan of salted water for about 10–15 minutes until tender, then drain and pat dry with paper towels.

5. Heat the oil for deep-frying in a deep saucepan to 340–350°F (see p.55) and deep-fry the potatoes until golden brown. Alternatively, you can rub the potatoes with a little oil, place on a baking sheet and cook under a hot grill for 3 minutes each side. Pat dry with paper towels and crush lightly to expose the flesh inside to the seasonings.

6. Mix the olive oil, garlic, thyme, lemon juice and salt and pepper to taste together in a bowl. Add the potatoes and leave them to sit for 10–15 minutes to absorb the flavors.

7. For the harissa aïoli, place the egg yolks, garlic and mustard in a blender and blend until well combined. Then while the blender is running, drizzle in the oils slowly. Do it slow, otherwise the aïoli will split — it's a good idea to keep taking breaks of a couple of seconds at a time from drizzling instead of maintaining a constant stream.

8. Once all the oil has been added, add the Harissa, lemon juice and salt to taste and blend for a few seconds until smooth. Transfer to a plastic squeezy bottle or piping bag.

9. To serve, smear a large platter or individual serving plates with a spoonful of Tapenade and place a potato in the center. Place 3 small dollops and 3 larger dollops of the harissa aïoli around the potato, then place the Fricassee buns on the small dollops (a little trick to prevent them from moving). Place 3 pieces of mackerel on each potato, then garnish the plates with the radishes, caperberries and quails' eggs. Place the Curly Scallions on top and drizzle over the Harissa oil.

For the cured mackerel

* ⅔ lb mackerel fillet (skinned and pin bones removed — ask your fishmonger to do the work for you)
* 1 cup Maldon salt flakes
* ¼ cup olive oil
* ¼ cup canola oil
* ½ tsp fennel seeds
* ½ tsp coriander seeds
* 1 star anise
* ½ tsp crushed red pepper flakes
* 1 sprig of thyme

For the new potatoes

* 4 new potatoes
* salt, to taste
* 1¼ cups canola oil, for deep-frying or just a little, for rubbing
* 4 tbsp olive oil
* 1 garlic clove, grated
* leaves from 1 sprig of thyme
* 2 tbsp freshly squeezed lemon juice
* pepper, to taste

For the harissa aïoli

* 2 egg yolks
* 1 garlic clove, peeled
* 1 Confit Garlic Clove (see p.46), optional
* 1 tsp mustard
* ⅔ cup canola oil
* 3 tbsp olive oil
* 1 tsp Harissa (see p.27)
* 1 tbsp freshly squeezed lemon juice
* salt, to taste

To serve

* 4 tbsp Tapenade (see p.35)
* 12 Fricassee mini buns (see p.234)
* 4 French radishes, thinly sliced and soaked in iced water
* 12 caperberries, cut in half lengthwise
* 4 quails' eggs, boiled for 3 minutes, then drained, cooled, peeled and cut in half
* Curly Scallions (see p.85)
* 4 tsp Harissa (see p.27)

Cured sardines or anchovies

by Yossi Elad

Makes 20

* 20 fresh sardines or anchovies, scaled, gutted, butterflied and deboned
* 4 tbsp high-quality coarse sea salt (I use Maldon salt)
* 2 sprigs of thyme, leaves picked
* ½ green chile, thinly sliced
* 1 ripe unwaxed lemon, sliced into rounds ¼ inch thick
* about 4¼ cups olive oil

I visited a friend who was recovering from a stroke and asked him if I could make anything for him to eat. The answer came, "I want four in a tin," and I responded, "Sardines?" He just smiled back at me.

Sardines and anchovies look very similar. Anchovies are a bit shinier and bluer. When I can get hold of fresh anchovies, I prefer them to sardines, but that's just me. Both are great. Ask your fishmonger to prepare them for you, but before you start curing these nice small fish, make sure you remove any remaining little bones — there is nothing more annoying than getting one stuck between your teeth.

1. In a sterilized 6½-cup airtight container (see p.24), arrange a layer of the sardines or anchovies and sprinkle with some of the salt, thyme leaves and chile. Cover with a layer of lemon slices. Continue layering in the same way until you have used up all the ingredients and the container is full.

2. Cover with the olive oil and seal the container. Leave for at least 10 hours in the fridge before serving. These can be kept in the fridge for up to 2 months, but just make sure that the fish are always covered with oil and that you take them out of the container with a clean utensil.

Yellowfin tuna tartare

With whipped sour cream,
Abadi-style savory cookies & schug

Serves 4

This is a really fun tartare that plays on texture and robust flavors. When we create a new dish for The Palomar we have a few goals in mind, the foremost of course being to make it super tasty and elegant, but also whimsical, interesting and original.

We start with the main star (the tuna), then find a few ingredients for supporting roles (here, the tomatoes, parsley, olive oil and lemon juice). Then we find the twist, and here we have three: the whipped cream for freshness and sourness; the Schug to complement the sour cream, but also to deliver a kick of spiciness, and finally the crushed Abadi cookies, which bring a surprising texture and are usually eaten at the end of a meal with a fresh glass of mint tea.

I chose yellowfin tuna for its texture and great taste, but you can also go for salmon, or red snapper if the fish is big and firm enough.

---

1. Start by whipping the sour cream with the sugar and a pinch of salt — it's a small amount, so you can whisk it by hand.

2. Mix the tuna, onion, tomatoes and parsley in a mixing bowl. Season to taste with salt and pepper and dress with the lemon juice and olive oil. Check to see whether you are happy with the seasoning and adjust if needed.

3. To serve, divide the sour cream between serving plates and smear with the tip of a spoon, just like an artistic chef. Repeat with the Schug on top, then place the tartare over that and garnish with a drizzle of olive oil and the crushed Abadi-style Savory Cookies.

* 6 tbsp sour cream
* pinch of sugar
* salt
* ⅔ lb yellowfin tuna, cut into ½-inch cubes (ask your fishmonger to give you loins closer to the head, which are less fatty and stringy)
* 1 small red onion, finely chopped
* 2 tomatoes, seeded and cut into ½-inch cubes
* generous handful of chopped parsley
* pepper, to taste
* 2 tbsp freshly squeezed lemon juice
* 3 tbsp olive oil, plus an extra drizzle to garnish
* 4 tbsp Schug (see p.34)
* 2–3 Abadi-style Savory Cookies (see p.237), roughly chopped, to serve

* ¼ cup fine bulgur wheat
* 4 tbsp just-boiled water
* salt
* ½ lb non-aged beef filet, trimmed of all fat and finely chopped (you can ask your butcher to trim it for you)
* 2 tbsp toasted pine nuts (see p.21)
* 2 tbsp freshly squeezed lemon juice
* 3 tbsp extra virgin olive oil
* cracked black pepper, to taste

For the flavor mix
* small handful of finely chopped parsley
* small handful of finely chopped cilantro
* small handful of finely chopped mint (don't go crazy with the chopping of this and the other herbs — chop them finely, but not to the point where they start to blacken)
* 1 tbsp finely chopped red onion
* 2 tbsp pomegranate seeds
* 1 tbsp ½-inch cubes of tomato (just the fleshy part; you could use the rest to make Velvet Tomatoes, see p.30)
* 2 tbsp freshly squeezed lemon juice
* 4–5 tbsp extra virgin olive oil
* salt, to taste
* 4 tbsp White Tahini Sauce (see p.28), to serve

Kubenia

Serves 4

Kubenia is the Lebanese way of making the famous steak tartare. The word kubenia *is actually a combination of two words in Arabic:* kibbeh, *meaning "ball," and* nayeh, *meaning "raw" — so "rawball!" (Yes, it does sound cooler in Arabic.) Traditionally it's made with finely chopped raw lamb, bulgur wheat, lemon juice and olive oil. I find the old-school version tasty yet a little too intense on the palate, so I've created a modern take using beef fillet. The "flavor mix" added to it (my own innovation; a kind of Israeli chimichurri) enriches the meat and blends with the tahini on the plate to create an irresistibly moppable sauce.*

---

1. For the tartare, put the bulgur wheat in a bowl, pour the 4 tablespoons of just-boiled water over and add a pinch of salt, then mix together (or follow the instructions on the package). Cover with plastic wrap and set aside until it has cooled completely. This can be done up to a day beforehand and the bulgur kept in the fridge. Once cooled, simply break up the bulgur with a fork to loosen it up and make it lighter.

2. In a bowl and using your (clean!) hands, mix the beef, bulgur, pine nuts, lemon juice, olive oil and some salt and cracked pepper together. Spend a good couple of minutes doing this — you need to break down the proteins in the meat and allow it to bond with the bulgur. Divide the mixture into quarters and form each quarter into a firm, oval-shaped ball.

3. Combine all the ingredients for the flavor mix in a bowl, seasoning to taste with salt.

4. To serve, put a spoonful of White Tahini Sauce in the center of each plate, place a tartare ball on top and spoon equal amounts of the flavor mix (dressing) over each. That's it! In the restaurant we pour the dressing over at the table, which gives the dish a fresher finish and more of a wow factor.

Beef carpaccio Yudale style

With asparagus, artichokes and truffle
Serves 4

This is the first beef carpaccio dish I created for Yudale, the crazy little brother across the street from our Machneyuda restaurant in Jerusalem, and it was so popular that it never came off the menu. Yudale has a special place in my heart as it was the first restaurant where I became head chef. This dish is packed with so many strong umami flavors that I get why it's addictive once you've tried it. Just make sure you use fresh non-aged beef.

As with all of our recipes, the easiest way is to work the processes in parallel.

1. First, preheat your oven to 350°F. Then on a baking sheet lined with a silicone mat (if you don't have one, parchment paper will do), divide the grated Parmesan into 4 thin rounds with enough space between each round to allow for them to spread a bit as you bake them. Bake for 3–4 minutes until golden and crisp, then leave to cool.

2. Meanwhile, if you're not using the aged stuff, reduce the balsamic vinegar and sugar in a pan over a low heat for 3–4 minutes until you have a syrupy consistency, then set aside to cool.

3. Blanch the asparagus in plenty of salted water for about 45 seconds (I like them crisp) and then plunge into iced water to stop the cooking.

4. Now for the fun part — take your anger out on the beef! Divide the slices into 4 batches, then place a flat layer of each batch with a little olive oil between 2 sheets of parchment paper and bang with a carpaccio hammer or meat tenderizing hammer until it's thin (if you don't have either of those, use a heavy-bottomed saucepan but just make sure you do it on a solid wood board to avoid smashing up your kitchen counter.

5. Now to the basil — this chopping method is called chiffonade. Place 4–5 leaves on top of each other, then roll and slice thinly with a sharp knife, which ensures that your basil stays green and is sliced evenly.

6. To serve, remove the top sheet of parchment paper from each batch of carpaccio and flip it meat-face-down on a serving plate, then remove the bottom sheet that has now become the top sheet. Season each carpaccio to taste with pepper and Maldon salt flakes. Add the onion, asparagus, artichokes and basil to each plate, then dress with the lemon juice, extra virgin olive oil, a touch of the balsamic and the truffle oil or some truffle shavings. Lastly, break up the Parmesan tuiles and scatter the pieces along with the walnuts over the plates.

* 2 cups Parmesan cheese, finely grated
* couple of drops of 10–20-year aged balsamic vinegar, or ¼ cup regular balsamic vinegar plus ½ tsp sugar (this is a neat little trick for those who don't have an expensive aged bottle at home, although I recommend making the investment, as it lasts for a long time and makes a huge difference)
* 4 asparagus spears, trimmed and cut into 1½–2-inch pieces
* salt
* ½ lb trimmed non-aged beef rump, thinly sliced against the grain
* olive oil, for oiling
* handful of basil leaves
* pepper, to taste
* Maldon salt flakes, to taste
* 2 tbsp finely chopped red onion
* 1 Roman artichoke or carciofo, sliced (the most addictive artichokes in the universe — I like to get mine straight from the source, i.e. Italian delis)
* 4 tsp freshly squeezed lemon juice
* 4–5 tbsp extra virgin olive oil
* couple of drops of good-quality white truffle oil for each serving (or if you have the extra cash and it's the right season, go for the real thing and dust with white truffle shavings)
* 2 tbsp toasted and chopped walnuts (see p.21)

Beef tartare with burned eggplant carpaccio, za'atar & tahini

Serves 4

* 2 eggplant, charred over an open flame and peeled (see p.51)
* 5 tbsp olive oil, plus extra for rubbing
* ⅔lb trimmed non-aged beef rump, finely chopped
* 2 small tomatoes, seeded and cut into ½-inch cubes
* 1 small red onion, finely chopped
* handful of chopped parsley
* 1 tsp sumac
* 1 tsp Za'atar Spice Mix (see p.20)
* salt and pepper, to taste
* 4 tbsp freshly squeezed lemon juice
* 2 tbsp toasted slivered almonds (see p.21)
* 4 tbsp tahini paste

I love the combination of smokiness and beef tartare, especially if it's rump, and what better companion than burned eggplant's creamy flesh? It has simple yet very strong flavors, goes well with beer, arak or whisky and, like most of the dishes in this book, really sings with some extra bread.

1. Start with the charred eggplant carpaccio. Divide the eggplant flesh between 4 10-inch squares of parchment paper, rubbed with a little olive oil. Cover each square with a second square of paper of the same size and flatten with your palm evenly.

2. Mix the beef, tomatoes, onion, parsley, sumac and Za'atar Spice Mix together in a bowl. Season to taste with salt and pepper, 2 tablespoons of the lemon juice and half the olive oil.

3. To serve, remove the top squares of parchment paper from each eggplant carpaccio, and flip them eggplant-face-down on a serving plate, then remove the bottom parchment. Season to taste with salt and pepper and the rest of the lemon juice and olive oil. Divide the tartare mixture between the plates, sprinkle with the slivered almonds and drizzle with the tahini paste.

Spring salad

Fennel and kohlrabi with poppy seeds & feta emulsion
Serves 4

The inspiration for this crunchy fresh salad is a much simpler dish called bishbash *(Moroccan for fennel). It's always on the table at my mama's house in springtime, and no matter how much she makes, it is always polished off. The original version combines just fennel, kohlrabi and carrot, and is seasoned with lemon juice, salt and olive oil. This version adds feta emulsion, poppy seeds and Watercress Pesto.*

1. To make the salad, slice the fennel bulbs thinly — I use a mandoline, but a sharp knife will also do; please watch your fingers.

2. Using a vegetable peeler, peel long ribbons from the kohlrabi and the asparagus stalks, then slice the asparagus tips with a knife. Plunge the fennel, kohlrabi and asparagus in plenty of iced water and leave for 30 minutes — this will ensure they are crispy. You can also do this ahead of time and leave them in the fridge for a couple of hours.

3. For the feta emulsion, blend all the ingredients in a powerful blender, then decant into a plastic squeezy bottle.

4. Drain the vegetables well — this is important because if there is still water on them the dressing won't coat them properly — and place in a mixing bowl.

5. Add the Watercress Pesto, poppy seeds, sunflower seeds, lemon juice and olive oil, season to taste with salt and mix very gently with your hands — imagine you're mixing fluffy clouds.

6. To serve, divide the salad between serving plates and dress with the feta emulsion on top. This salad is best eaten straight away so that you can enjoy optimum crunchiness.

For the salad

* 2 fennel bulbs
* 1 large kohlrabi, peeled
* 6 fat asparagus spears, peeled and trimmed
* 2 tbsp Watercress Pesto (see p.31)
* 1 tbsp poppy seeds
* 1 tbsp toasted sunflower seeds
* 2 tbsp freshly squeezed lemon juice
* 3 tbsp olive oil
* salt, to taste

For the feta emulsion

* 3 oz feta cheese
* 1 tsp white wine vinegar
* ⅓ cup water
* 1 tbsp olive oil

Grazia's tomato salad

Serves 4

We make this salad exactly how my grandma Grazia used to make it. It's spicy and sour, and totally addictive. I like to have it with merguez sausages, but it also works really well with fish and seafood. Just make sure to pair it with a strongly flavored protein — one that can put up a good fight in the face of the intensity of this salad. When all's said and done, my favorite way to eat it is simply with some plain white rice.

———

Mix all the ingredients together in a bowl, let the salad to sit for 5–10 minutes and garnish with a few chile slices before serving.

* 7–8 firm tomatoes, cut into ½-inch cubes (keep all the juice/pulp that is left on the chopping board from cutting — that's the secret of this salad!)
* 1 large green chile, seeded and finely chopped (include the seeds if you like it extra hot), plus a few slices to garnish
* 1 unwaxed lemon, first sliced into rounds ½ inch thick, then seeded and cut into ½-inch cubes, including the rind
* 1 bunch of cilantro, roughly chopped
* 1 small red onion, chopped into small cubes
* 2 tbsp freshly squeezed lemon juice
* ¼ cup olive oil
* salt, to taste

Tomer's grandma Grazia Ben-Yeshaya, 1933

For the caramelized walnuts

* ¼ cup granulated sugar
* ½ cup toasted walnuts, about 2 handfuls (see p.21)

For the citrus vinaigrette

* 1 small garlic clove, peeled
* 2 Garlic Confit Cloves (see p.46), optional
* ¼ cup freshly squeezed orange juice
* 1 tbsp freshly squeezed lemon juice
* 1 tsp date syrup
* 1 tsp Dijon mustard
* pinch of salt
* 4 tbsp canola oil
* 2 tbsp olive oil

* 1 head of chicory
* 1 small mild radicchio (or ¼ large one)
* ½ frisée lettuce (curly endive)
* 1 Granny Smith apple, cored and thinly sliced
* 6–7 Medjool dates, pitted and hand torn (try to buy good-quality soft ones)
* 3½ oz blue Stilton cheese, crumbled
* salt, to taste

A date with chicory & blue Stilton salad

Serves 4

I love salads that balance savory and sweet, and what a great leaf chicory (also called endive, or Belgian endive) is for that mission. This bitter lettuce grows in the dark and is also known as "white gold." For this recipe, I took inspiration from the classic Waldorf salad (the walnuts and the apples) and gave it a Palomar twist. The citrus vinaigrette is excellent with any leafy salad, especially with more bitter leaves like frisée (curly endive), radicchio or arugula, so feel free to do your own thing with it.

———

1. For the caramelized walnuts, heat a heavy-bottomed nonstick pan over a low heat and add the sugar in one even layer. Don't stir or move the pan, as the sugar will recrystallize if you do and we don't want that, love! Once all the sugar has melted and you have a nice brown caramel, take the pan off the heat, stir in the walnuts and then transfer to a tray lined with parchment paper. Let cool.

2. Once the walnuts are completely cooled, blitz in a blender using a couple of pulses. Set aside. These can be prepared a day or two ahead, as they will keep for a week in an airtight container.

3. For the citrus vinaigrette, put all the ingredients except the oils in a blender and blend until smooth. Then while continuing to blend, add the oils gradually to create an emulsion. The vinaigrette can be kept in an airtight container in the fridge for 4 days.

4. To prepare the salad, trim the bottom of the chicory and separate the leaves — you will need to repeat this process until all the leaves have been freed. Then do the same with the radicchio. Trim the frisée — I like to trim away all the thick white parts — then wash and dry all the leaves.

5. Place the leaves in a large bowl and add two-thirds of the apple, dates, Stilton and caramelized walnuts. Season to taste with salt and the vinaigrette. A good tip is never to add all the dressing at once, you want the ingredients just coated and no more, and adding is easy — taking out, well, that's a different story. Mix with your hands like you're mixing clouds, in a very airy and gentle manner; we want the leaves to stay light and crunchy.

6. To serve, divide the salad among 4 serving plates or transfer to one big bowl and garnish with the rest of the apple, dates, Stilton and caramelized walnuts. As with all leafy salads, it's better to eat this as soon as you've dressed it.

Fattoush salad

Serves 4

Bread-based salads are such a smart use of stale bread, and mixing it with fresh ingredients brings out the best in both. This Levantine star is no exception. The ingredients in this salad vary from season to season, but usually contain tomatoes, cucumbers, onion and sumac. This version has a Palomar twist, bringing a fantastic combination of textures and flavors.

———

1. Start by making the croutons, as they need time to cool before you make the salad. Preheat your oven to 325°F. Toss the bread cubes with the olive oil, Za'atar Spice Mix and some salt until evenly coated. Tip on to a baking sheet and bake for 12–15 minutes — we want them crispy and crunchy. Let cool completely.

I prepare a big batch of these at home and keep them in an airtight container; if they are done properly and are really dry and crispy, they will easily keep for up to a week.

2. Place the croutons with all the salad ingredients except the Labneh, Za'atar and Brazil nuts in a mixing bowl, season to taste with salt and pepper and mix well. It should taste quite sour, so don't be shy about adding extra lemon juice if needed.

3. To serve, divide the Labneh among 4 serving plates (or go for one big one). Make a nice dimple in the middle of the cheese and season with the Za'atar Spice Mix. Place the salad center stage, then garnish with the chopped Brazil nuts and an extra drizzle of olive oil over the Labneh.

For the croutons

* 2 slices of stale Challah (see p.238, or any kind of bread or pita), cut into ½-inch cubes
* 2–3 tbsp olive oil
* 1 tsp Za'atar Spice Mix (see p.20)
* salt, to taste

* 4 good-quality tomatoes, cut into 1-inch cubes, or 1⅔ cups good-quality cherry tomatoes, halved
* 4 baby Dutch cucumbers or 2 English (regular) ones, halved lengthwise, then cut into slices ½ inch thick
* 1 red onion, halved and sliced
* handful of roughly chopped parsley leaves
* handful of roughly chopped mint leaves
* 1 tbsp sumac
* 1½ tbsp Tapenade (see p.35)
* 3 tbsp freshly squeezed lemon juice, or to taste
* 3 tbsp olive oil, plus an extra drizzle to garnish
* salt and pepper, to taste
* 4 tbsp Labneh (see p.41)
* 1 tbsp Za'atar Spice Mix (see p.20)
* 4 tbsp toasted and chopped Brazil nuts (see p.21), to garnish

THE MAIN ACT

We're finally at the main act, so heat up your oven, fire up your stove, sharpen your knives and let's get ready to cook. Everything you have created so far will have prepared you for this moment. The Harissa, Cured Lemons and Watercress Pesto (and much more) are going to come into full use now.

What is great about this chapter is that almost every dish contains two or three recipes that stand alone as excellent side dishes. We have included as many variations as possible so that you can experiment even further and develop your skills in the cooking of modern-day Jerusalem.

We are bringing the very best that The Palomar has to offer: recipes that use interesting but not too expensive ingredients and loads of vegetables, herbs and proteins, with a nice emphasis on my personal favorite: offal. For some reason, offal gets a bad rap. I know that it is not the simplest of ingredients, but it is really tasty, healthy and most of the time fairly easy to cook — just keep an open mind.

by Tomer Amedi

Shakshuka two ways

Shakshuka (meaning "to shake" or "a mixture") is simply a dish of eggs poached in a tomato, pepper, garlic and chile stew. However, for me, shakshuka is a way of living, a philosophy if you like.

Originating from Tripoli, Tunisia, this breakfast/brunch dish is popular right across the Maghreb region and was first brought to Israel in the 1950s by Jews migrating from that area. Because it's so easy to make and has eggs in it, it became a huge favorite for breakfast, brunch and even dinner (hell, I'll have it for lunch as well if you'll give me the chance).

I was 13 years old when my mama went away for a whole month to visit my older brother in Chicago, so it was just Papa and me. The first week was OK, as Mama had left 3 tons of food in the fridge and life was easy. The second week I started to cook a bit, but it was hard, and I didn't know many recipes at that time. My papa was working late every night, so I started to cook bigger and bigger batches to save having to cook every single day when I came back from school. One night he came home from work, and we both agreed we were tired of eating the same zucchinis from yesterday and the day before. Having seen my desperation, he put his cooking skills into action (and he is a great cook). "Watch and learn, son," he said with a sparkle in his eyes. Pan on the burner, old zucchini stew in, bit of water, chop chop chop some herbs, break in four eggs, shake the pan once or twice, turn the heat low, season a bit and bang. Dinner ready in 7 minutes! I was blown away — even my mama doesn't cook that fast and she's a Tasmanian devil! It was heavenly. He handed me some Challah and declared: "As long as you have two eggs and some bread to mop, you'll always have a meal in 10 minutes."

And that's the real philosophy behind shakshuka. Everybody can make it easily with very few ingredients or yesterday's leftovers. Shakshuka reinvents itself every time you make it and surprises you when all hope of a proper meal has been lost.

And now for my interpretations of easy, quick and healthy shakshuka.

———

Fast traditional shakshuka

Serves 4

For this traditional take you are allowed to cheat a bit and use our Matbucha recipe with a little more liquid and herbs, or the Chraymeh sauce recipe.

———

1. Heat your chosen sauce in a large, wide, shallow pan, stirring in the water — you need to start with a loose sauce, as some of the liquid will evaporate during the cooking.

2. Season to taste with salt, then break the eggs into the sauce, one by one, making sure that you keep the yolks whole. Drag the egg whites a bit with a fork to allow them to mix slightly with the sauce. This will ensure that the flavor is spread evenly through your shakshuka.

3. Simmer over a very low heat for 10–15 minutes until the egg whites set nicely but the yolks are still runny. I always go for a runny yolk — nothing beats that buttery sensation in your mouth — but I know some people like their yolks cooked through, so if you belong to that school, simply cover the pan during the cooking process.

4. Season the yolks with salt and pepper, sprinkle with the chopped parsley, make sure the bread is not too far away and dig in! I like to eat this straight from the pan and therefore wait for everybody to take theirs so that I can be last and keep the best bits to myself. Try it and you'll see exactly what I mean, but just keep this information to yourself or you'll need to fight for it. Been there, done that.

* 1 recipe of Matbucha (see p.52) or Chraymeh sauce (see p.145) (use as is if you already have some in your fridge, but if preparing fresh, cook over a high heat in half the time — the shakshuka won't mind!)
* 1–2 cups water
* salt, to taste
* 8 eggs (I serve 2 eggs per person, but you can go for more or fewer)
* pepper, to taste
* handful of chopped parsley, to garnish

New-style shakshuka

Serves 4

* salt
* 1 small cauliflower, broken into 1¼–2-inch evenly sized florets
* ¼ cup olive oil
* 1 eggplant, cut into ¾-inch cubes
* pepper
* ½ tsp crushed red pepper flakes
* 1 tbsp toasted and ground cumin seeds
* 1 tsp toasted and ground coriander seeds (optional)
* 2–3 garlic cloves, sliced, or very finely chopped (depending on how intense you like your garlic)
* handful of fresh oregano leaves
* ¾ cup vegetable stock (see p.123 for homemade), or water
* 1 zucchini, shaved into ribbons with a peeler
* 8 eggs
* handful of chopped parsley, to garnish

1. Place a large pan of water on the burner with 2 tablespoons salt added and bring to a boil. Blanch the cauliflower florets for 2–3 minutes, then drain and set aside.

2. Meanwhile, heat a large pan over a medium-high heat, add the oil and then the eggplant cubes. Now this is important: make sure you season every ingredient that goes in the pan with some salt and pepper and a little of the crushed red pepper flakes, cumin and coriander (if using) to ensure that your shakshuka bursts with flavor — you can mix the dried spices (but not the salt) together to make them easier to add.

3. Cook the eggplant for about 5–7 minutes until they have a nice golden color. Then add the cauliflower florets, garlic and oregano, season as before and cook, stirring, for 3–4 minutes.

4. Crank up the heat, add the stock or water and scrape the base of the pan with a wooden spoon (that's where all the flavor is) to deglaze. Let the stock to boil for 30 seconds, then add the zucchini shavings and the rest of the spices. Break the eggs gently into the sauce and drag the egg whites (see step 2 of Fast Traditional Shakshuka, left).

5. Lower the heat and cook for about 10–15 minutes until the whites have set but the yolks are still runny. Season the yolks with salt and pepper, sprinkle with the chopped parsley and rock on.

Variations

As I have said, you can reinvent this dish every time you make it, so try using boiled potato cubes, blanched green beans, black olives, bacon, ham, chorizo, feta cheese, ricotta cheese, shaved celeriac, some fresh skinned and quartered tomatoes or the Velvet Tomatoes (see p.30), Zucchini Machluta (see p.74), Salata Mashwiya (see p.77) or any old stew or cooked vegetable you have as leftovers from yesterday's main meal. The possibilities are endless once you get the gist of it. Just be as creative as you can.

Cauliflower steak with Labneh & grated tomatoes

Serves 4

Along with eggplant, I think cauliflower is one of the "meatiest" vegetables out there. It's so rich in texture and flavor that I like to glorify it and give it the center stage. Baking it as big steaks helps to keep its natural flavor intense yet bright, and makes the most of that firm, "meaty" texture.

---

1. Preheat your oven to 400°F. Place the cauliflower halves, cut-side down, on a baking sheet. Mix the stock or water with the melted butter and drizzle over the cauliflower, then give them a good rub. Season with some salt and sugar and the crushed red pepper flakes. Cover with foil and bake for 45 minutes–1 hour, or until the cauliflower is easy to pierce with a knife but not too soft; I recommend that you check it after 45 minutes.

2. Meanwhile, mix all the ingredients for the grated tomatoes together in a bowl and set aside. Do the same with the cured lemon butter ingredients.

3. Once the cauliflower is ready, take it out of the oven and heat your grill to its highest setting. Rub the cauliflower with the cured lemon butter and grill for 5–7 minutes until golden brown. (The reason we don't add the cured lemon butter from the start is to avoid it becoming bitter.)

4. To serve, place a spoonful of Labneh on each serving plate and season with the Za'atar Spice Mix, then place the cauliflower on top, spoon the grated tomatoes on top of that and garnish with the slivered almonds, parsley and Maldon salt flakes.

* 2 small or medium cauliflowers, halved
* ¼ cup vegetable stock (see p.123 for homemade) or water
* 2 tbsp butter, melted
* salt, to taste
* sugar, to taste
* pinch of crushed red pepper flakes

For the grated tomatoes

* 2 ripe tomatoes, grated (discard the skins)
* 1 garlic clove, finely grated
* pinch of cumin seeds
* drizzle of olive oil
* salt, to taste

For the cured lemon butter

* 2 tbsp butter, melted
* 1 tbsp Cured Lemon Paste (see p.25)
* 1 tsp ground almonds

To garnish

* 4 tbsp Labneh (see p.41)
* 1 tsp Za'atar Spice Mix (see p.20)
* handful of toasted slivered almonds (see p.21)
* handful of chopped parsley
* sprinkle of Maldon salt flakes

Vegetable stock

Makes 12 cups

In the restaurant, we use vegetable stock like water, adding it to almost everything we cook. In my opinion it's the essence of fresh, flavorful cooking, and it keeps the food light. I'd be lying if I said I used vegetable stock every time I cook at home, but when I do, it always tastes better! It's a great base for any soups, risottos or stews you're making, so it's always good to have some on hand. Worst case, just chop whatever vegetables you have in the fridge, boil, add salt and you've got a healthy tasty soup in 15 minutes. A good tip when you're cooking other recipes is to save the vegetable trimmings, such as onion, carrot and so on, give them a good wash and add to the stock, then nothing goes to waste.

* 1 white onion, cut into quarters
* 1 small leek (including green part), cut into 6 lengths and well washed
* 1 large carrot, cut into 5 lengths
* 2–3 celery ribs, cut into quarters
* 1 bunch of parsley sprigs
* 3 sprigs of thyme
* 1 bay leaf
* 16 cups cold water

1. Put all the ingredients in a large pan (a 5½-quart one is good), bring to a boil and then simmer gently for an hour, by which time the stock should be lightly colored and flavorful.

2. Strain the stock and leave to cool. What to do with the leftover vegetables? They gave up all their flavor to the water, poor things, so they will taste rather bland at this stage. But all is not lost — revived with some salt and pepper and fresh olive oil, they make a nice nibble, especially when they're still hot.

3. Once cooled, the stock can be kept in the fridge in an airtight container, for up to 48 hours, or you can freeze it in 1-cup or 2-cup containers to be used as needed.

Polenta Jerusalem style

Serves 4

"What's Jerusalem style?" is the oft-repeated question. In fact, there's no particular Jerusalemite ingredient here — the name honors the story of how this unassuming little pot became our signature dish. When we opened Machneyuda, we were missing one final hot starter for the menu. Assaf (the undisputed polenta maestro) suggested we knock up a polenta dish, and despite some resistance from Uri (who later had to eat his words…), we went along with it. Service began, and before we knew it we were being blitzed with polenta orders. Half an hour in and we were clean out of plates. Casting around for ideas, Assaf grabbed a pickle jar and said, "How 'bout this?" Well, it was a smash! People went nuts for the jar — it kept the polenta warm and when you lifted the lid you were hit with the heavenly aromas of truffle and Parmesan. There is something universal about comfort food, the way it takes you in its arms and gives you a warm, fuzzy hug — it immediately transports us to that cozy childhood place of safety and indulgence. That's what this dish is all about.

―――――

The easiest and fastest approach to this recipe is to work on each element in parallel. So prep all your ingredients first and it'll be a breeze.

1. For the asparagus, bring a small saucepan of salted water to a boil for blanching the asparagus. At the same time, set over a medium heat both a shallow, heavy-bottomed pan for the mushroom ragout and a large saucepan for the polenta.

2. For the mushroom ragout, add the butter to the ragout pan and then the mushrooms. The ragout will now more or less look after itself — you just need to give it a stir occasionally.

3. For the polenta, pour the milk and cream into the large saucepan, bring to a simmer and then gradually add the polenta, whisking constantly. This is the most important process, so give it your undivided attention and don't stop whisking. Once you've added all the polenta, continue to whisk over a low heat for 15–20 minutes until it thickens. The thicker it gets, the more lava-like it becomes — all bubbly and jumpy. Whisk in the butter and Parmesan, season to taste with salt, then remove from the heat. By now your mushroom ragout should have become darker in color and almost dry. Time to season it to taste with salt and pepper. If you feel the polenta is a bit "heavy" feel free to add a bit of water.

4. Your water should now be boiling, so toss in the asparagus and blanch for about 30–45 seconds (I like it to retain a good bite). Remove and dress with a drizzle of olive oil and squeeze of lemon juice, then season to taste with salt and pepper.

5. To serve, divide the polenta between 4 jam jars or other preserving jars, add the ragout, top with the asparagus and finish with the shaved Parmesan and a drizzle of truffle oil. Close the jar and wait for 30 seconds… and…

For the asparagus

* salt
* 4 asparagus spears, peeled, trimmed and cut into thirds
* drizzle of olive oil
* squeeze of lemon juice
* grind of pepper

For the mushroom ragout

* 2 tbsp butter
* ⅔ lb button mushrooms, torn
* ½ lb chestnut mushrooms, torn
* salt and pepper, to taste

Variation

Sometimes I like to add chopped crispy bacon (everything tastes better with bacon, no?), and if you really want to go to town, add a poached egg.

For the polenta

* 1½ cups milk
* 1½ cups light cream or half-and-half
* ⅔ cup polenta (I use polenta bramata per polenta gialla, which gives a rich golden color, alternatively use any good-quality polents, but not the instant type)
* 1½ tbsp unsalted butter
* small handful of grated Parmesan cheese
* salt, to taste

To garnish

* generous handful of shaved Parmesan cheese
* drizzle of good-quality truffle oil

Eggplant & Feta Bourekas
See p.128–9

Eggplant & feta bourekas

Serves 4

To this day, no one knows who invented bourekas: the Turks or the Bulgarians (I think it was the Turks, but don't tell my Bulgarian friends). This crispy puff pastry is usually filled with cheese, mashed potatoes or spinach, and it's my favorite Friday morning brunch dish. In Machane Yehuda market you can buy them hot in a takeout box and I can easily get through a whole one by myself. It's definitely my Kryptonite! When you really want to make it special, add some hard-boiled eggs, tahini and brine pickles, and you have what we call a pampering feast. I took an extra step here and created an open-style boureka filled with Swiss chard, eggplant and feta. Feel free to play with the filling any way you want.

Before you begin, it's important to make sure if using frozen pastry that you defrost it in the fridge, otherwise the butter in it will melt and instead of puff pastry you will have a mess. Also remember to work with the pastry in a cold room.

1. To make the bourekas, preheat your oven to 400°F and line a baking sheet with parchment paper. Cut the square sheet of pastry diagonally across in both directions to create 4 triangles, then place them on the lined baking sheet.

2. Brush with the egg wash and sprinkle with the sesame seeds. Bake for 17–20 minutes until golden and puffed. Set aside. (You can bake the bourekas close to your serving time or in advance and reheat — either way works fine.) Leave the oven on.

3. To make the Swiss chard stew, heat a saucepan over a medium heat, add the oil and butter and sauté the onion. Meanwhile, dice the white stalks of the Swiss chard and add them to the pot, then roughly chop the green leafy parts.

4. Once the onion and stalks have softened, add the garlic and some salt, and sauté for another 2 minutes, then add the spinach and the green leafy parts of the Swiss chard.

5. Now for the fun bit — you don't touch the stew until it's the right moment. And when is that? When the greens have reduced their volume by two-thirds, which takes around 20 minutes. Only then can you stir and cook for an extra 10–15 minutes before seasoning to taste with salt and the lemon juice — we want most of the liquid to vaporize. This stew is great with so many recipes — I use it for the Mussels Hamusta (see p.142) and the Seared Scallops with Cured Lemon Beurre Blanc (see p.132), but you can also add it to pastas, omelettes, stews and soups, or have it as a side with some cheese on top; it's very versatile and incredibly tasty.

6. To prepare the eggplant for the filling, heat up the oil in a skillet and fry the eggplant slices, flipping them from time to time, until they get a nice golden brown color on both sides. Transfer to a tray lined with plenty of paper towels and season to taste with salt and the cumin while still hot.

For the bourekas

* 5½-in square, ¼-inch thick, of good-quality all-butter puff pastry (if you've bought a larger quantity, you can freeze the rest, or use to make a larger quantity of bourekas and freeze, then any time you have a craving for them you can have them in a trice — it's a craving that never goes away, just waiting for a moment of weakness)
* 1 egg, beaten, for egg wash
* 1 tbsp sesame seeds

For the Swiss chard stew

* 4 tsp olive oil
* 2 tbsp butter
* 1 onion, finely chopped
* 1 small bunch of Swiss chard, washed, white stalks and leafy green parts separated
* 1 garlic clove, finely chopped
* salt, to taste
* 1lb spinach, washed
* 2 tbsp freshly squeezed lemon juice

For the filling

* ¾ cup canola oil
* 1 eggplant, sliced into rounds
  ¾ inch thick
* salt, to taste
* ½ tsp toasted and ground
  cumin seeds
* 4 oz feta cheese
* 4 tbsp raw tahini paste

For the garnish

* 4 tbsp Labneh (see p.41),
  mixed with 1 tsp amba (cured
  mango paste/sauce) or amchur
  (dried mango) powder (optional
  — you can use Indian mango
  pickle mixed with a bit of
  Hawaij Spice Mix, see p. 20,
  or ground turmeric if you can't
  find amba)
* 2 hard-boiled eggs, peeled
  and halved
* salt and pepper, to taste
* 2 pickles in brine, halved
* 4 tsp Harissa (see p.27)
* 1 bunch of micro cilantro
  (optional)

7. To assemble, smear a bit of the Labneh mix on each serving plate. While still on the hot side, cut the bourekas horizontally through the middle (like a bagel) so that you have a top and a bottom part. Place the bottom part on each plate.

8. Organize 4 stacks on a baking sheet lined with parchment paper, each stack consisting of 2 layers of eggplant, Swiss chard stew (make sure you drain off some of the liquid) and feta cheese, then heat them up in the oven, still set to 400°F for 3–4 minutes.

9. Place the stacks on the boureka bases, drizzle with the raw tahini paste and sandwich with the top halves of the bourekas.

10. Place a hard-boiled egg half on each plate and season to taste with salt and pepper, then a pickle half and a drizzle of Harissa oil. Finally, garnish with the micro cilantro, if available.

Papi's spinach gnocchi

by Yossi Elad
Serves 3–4

* 1lb spinach, stalks removed
* 1 cup ricotta cheese
* salt, to taste
* 3 tbsp all-purpose flour
* ¾ cup butter
* 2¼ cups goats' yogurt
* ¼ tsp freshly grated nutmeg

I was walking along an alley in Praiano in the Campania region of Italy when through the kitchen window of a small house I saw an Italian Mama working with dumplings. So I asked her, "Che cosa fai?" ("What are you doing?"). The Mama invited me in and said that she was preparing gnocchi di spinaci con ricotta. *She went on to explain to me, "Take the spinach and steam it, then squeeze all the liquid out, add flour, egg, salt and finally the ricotta. Then place the fresh gnocchi in the tomato sauce." I can tell you, it tasted like heaven!*

Some time later in our restaurant, the smell of freshly chopped spinach brought the memory flooding back. I took her recipe but this time didn't squeeze all the liquid from the spinach, melted some butter and added goats' yogurt, let it simmer slowly and then put the gnocchi in the simmering yogurt. This tasted like heaven, too!

1. Wash the spinach and pat it dry with paper towels. Chop it finely, then add the ricotta cheese, salt to taste and flour and mix together until it has a smooth texture. Cover and chill in the fridge for 30 minutes.

2. Melt the butter in a saucepan over a medium-low heat, add the yogurt and slowly bring to a simmer, making sure the sauce doesn't split. Season with the grated nutmeg.

3. Shape the spinach mixture into small oval shapes — use 2 wet tablespoons to help you to achieve a neat shape — and drop them gently, one at a time as you shape them, straight into the sauce.

4. Cook for 2 minutes, again making sure you simmer slowly, otherwise the sauce will split.

5. To serve, arrange the gnocchi in serving dishes and add 3–4 spoonfuls of the warm yogurt sauce on top.

Seared scallops with cured lemon beurre blanc

Serves 4

This is the first scallop dish I created for The Palomar. In Jerusalem, good-quality fresh scallops are very hard to come by, so I was excited to be able to work with them in London. This dish says everything about why I love my job: you take some great local ingredients, use French technique, infuse it with some old-school home flavors and create something new. Add Yael's crispy Hazelnut Tuiles and you're the happiest chef alive!

I know, this looks like a lot of prep, but if you do it all simultaneously it will take you less than an hour, which isn't bad for a restaurant-quality dish. Try to kick them all off at the same time and you'll get the hang of it. Another option, if you'd like to get ahead, is to prepare the Swiss chard, artichokes, the base for the beurre blanc (you can make a double batch of this and keep it in the fridge) and the tuiles a day before and then just heat them up and sear the scallops on the day. Which means 7 minutes and it's on the table.

---

1. For the cured lemon beurre blanc, heat a saucepan over a medium heat, add ½ tbsp of the butter and sauté the shallots with the thyme and star anise until soft.

2. Add the white wine and reduce by half, then add the vinegar and reduce by half again. Add the stock and… again reduce by half. Pick out the star anise, then add the Cured Lemon Paste and the cream and bring to a boil.

3. Take off the heat and blitz in a blender or food processor until smooth, then pass through a fine sieve. As the great chef Thomas Keller once said, "When in doubt, sieve!"

4. Pour the sauce back into the pan (having given it a good rinse first), heat to a simmer and then whisk in the remaining butter. Take off the heat, season to taste with salt, and the white pepper if you like, and set aside.

5. For the Jerusalem artichokes, preheat your oven to 425°F. Drain the artichokes and pat dry, then place with the rest of the ingredients in an ovenproof dish or deep baking sheet, seasoning to taste with salt and pepper. Cover with foil and bake for 40 minutes. Remove from the oven and leave, covered, for 5–10 minutes.

6. For the scallops. When everything else is hot and ready, and the tuiles have cooled and are ready to use, place a large pan on the burner and get it piping-hot. Make sure your scallops are nice and dry (watery scallops + hot oil = trouble), and season them with salt and pepper.

For the cured lemon beurre blanc

* ¼ cup cold butter, cut into cubes
* 2 shallots, diced
* 1–2 tsp chopped thyme
* 1 star anise
* 3 tbsp white wine
* 2 tbsp white wine vinegar
* 2 tbsp vegetable stock (see p.123 for homemade) or fish stock or water
* 1 tbsp Cured Lemon Paste (see p.25)
* 2 tsp heavy cream
* salt, to taste
* pinch of white pepper (optional)

For the Jerusalem artichokes

* ⅔ lb peeled Jerusalem artichokes, cut into rounds ½ inch thick or cut in half if they're small — keep in water until you cook them
* 2 tbsp white wine
* 2 tbsp vegetable stock (see p.123 for homemade) or water
* 1 tsp chopped thyme
* 1 tbsp butter, cut into cubes
* salt and pepper, to taste

For the scallops

* 12 fresh scallops, cleaned
  (if you can get hand-dived ones,
  they will be awesome)
* salt and pepper
* 2 tbsp canola oil
* 1 tbsp olive oil
* ¼ cup butter
* 2 tbsp freshly squeezed
  lemon juice

To serve

* 4 large tbsp Swiss Chard Stew (see
  p.128), hot and ready for action
* 4 4-inch square Hazelnut Tuiles
  made without sugar (see p.200)

7. Add both oils to the pan, then the scallops, one by one, and sear until you see a nice golden brown halo on the bottom. Flip them over, add the butter and, using a spoon, baste the scallops with it, loving and pampering them — this is my favorite cooking technique, called *arrosage* in French.

8. When the scallops have a nice golden brown color, add the lemon juice and then remove them from the pan straight on to paper towels. They should be firm yet bouncy to the touch.

9. To serve, spoon the Swiss Chard Stew on to the serving plates and top with the Jerusalem artichokes. Place the scallops on top, dress around with the beurre blanc and top with the Hazelnut Tuiles.

Papi's polpo

by Yossi Elad

For 1 octopus

I was once walking on the beach and in the distance I spotted a group of fishermen with piles of fish next to them. Not far from where they were standing was an older fisherman holding something in his hands and smacking it against the rocks. I just had to ask him what he was doing and he simply answered, "I caught a polpo." "But why are you smacking it on the rocks?" I inquired, to which he replied, "It softens the meat." So I now know various legends about softening octopus, from cooking it with a wine cork to smacking it against rocks.

---

1. Freeze your sea creature for 24 hours, then defrost it, which will help to tenderize it.

2. Preheat your oven to 300°F. Put the octopus on a baking sheet and add the rest of the ingredients except the red wine. Cover the baking sheet with parchment paper and then foil.

3. Cook the octopus in the oven for 1½ hours.

4. Increase the oven temperature to 325°F and cook for another 1½ hours — don't add any liquid.

5. When you unveil the octopus, you will see that it's swimming in its own juices. If, however, you want an octopus with a dark red color, add some red wine for the last 20 minutes of the cooking time. Take the beast out of the tray and leave it to cool. You can now use it for making the Octo-hummus (see p.138) or any other dish you want.

* 1¾ lb – 2¼ lb octopus, inside cleaned (Spanish ones are great)
* 2 small onions, cut in half
* 1 tomato, cut into quarters
* 1 tsp black peppercorns
* 1 small unwaxed orange, cut into quarters
* 2 bay leaves
* 2 sprigs of thyme
* 1 unwaxed lemon, cut in half
* 1 unwaxed lime, cut in half (optional)
* 1 leek, sliced (optional)
* a few leafy celery ribs (optional)
* generous glug of red wine (optional)

_____ **The ultimate aim of civility and good manners is to please: to please one's guest and one's host. To this end one uses the rules strictly laid down by tradition: of welcome, generosity, affability, cheerfulness and consideration for others.**
Claudia Roden

Octo-hummus
See p.138-9

Octo-hummus

Serves 6

"It sounds like the name of Spider-Man's nemesis," Uri said with a wink, but I like to think the octopus is actually the superhero of this dish. Octopus is one of those ingredients that looks a bit intimidating, but once you get the hang of it, it's pretty simple to work with; it's all about the tenderizing of the beast. You can go the extra mile with creating the steak shape, which gives this dish the wow factor, but it will taste just as good if you chop the tentacles roughly. In the restaurant, we use a Josper charcoal oven to achieve the smoky flavor; at home, an outdoor charcoal barbecue will do the trick. Needless to say, the Baba Ganoush, or eggplant hummus, can be enjoyed as a great hot or cold mezze in its own right. The same applies to the chickpea masabacha (a traditional hummus topping), and the tomato confit is great for pastas or grilled fish or meat.

If you decide to create the steak shape, you will need to start preparing the octopus a day ahead. It sounds like a lot to do, but if you work efficiently, the process is fast and easy. Just make sure everything is ready in advance.

1. For the octopus, first follow Papi's method for preparing the octopus on p.134.

2. If you are going for steaks, make sure you work with a warmish octopus. Place a double layer of plastic wrap on a chopping board, but leave the plastic wrap attached to the roll. Separate the tentacles from the head (discard the inside of the head and the beak). Place 4 tentacles in a row, thick part on your left-hand side. Slice up the head and lay the slices on top of the tentacles. On top of this, lay the other 4 tentacles, thick part on your right hand side. Start rolling up the octopus tightly in the plastic wrap into a sausage shape, using as much plastic wrap as you need. With each rolling motion, squeeze the air out to the sides (imagine you're stretching the tentacles).

3. Once it is all tightly rolled up poke a few holes in the plastic wrap with a skewer — we need all the air to be released from the sausage so that it will be nice and tight. Wipe the sausage with damp paper towels to clean it, then wrap again with more plastic wrap. Chill in the fridge overnight and then cut into 6 steaks, then remove the plastic wrap. Alternatively, go freestyle and just roughly chop the octopus.

4. To make the tomato confit, preheat your oven to 275°F. Place all the ingredients in a deep but small baking sheet (make sure your babies are nicely submerged in the oil) and bake for 2–3 hours.

5. Remove from the oven and let cool. You can store the confit in the fridge for up to a week — transfer to a sterilized airtight container or jar and keep covered with oil. (When I make this at home, I do a double batch and then also use the oil separately — it's great for pastas and fish.)

For the octopus

* 1 recipe of Papi's Polpo (see p.134)
* 6 heaping tbsp Baba Ganoush (see p.51)

For the tomato confit

* 18 cherry tomatoes
* 1 garlic clove, peeled
* ½ green chile
* ½ cup olive oil
* salt, to taste

For the parsley dressing

* ½ bunch of parsley
* 1 tbsp Cured Lemon Paste (see p.25)
* 1 garlic clove, peeled
* 3 tbsp freshly squeezed lemon juice
* pinch of toasted and ground cumin seeds
* salt, to taste
* ¼ cup olive oil
* ¼ cup canola oil

For the chickpea masabacha

* 1 cup dried chickpeas, soaked in 8½ cups cold water overnight
* ½ tsp baking soda
* 1 garlic clove, peeled
* ½ green chile, tail trimmed but left whole
* 1 tsp Jerusalem Spice Mix (see p.18)
* handful of chopped parsley
* handful of chopped coriander
* squeeze of lemon juice
* 1 tbsp Parsley Dressing (see opposite)
* salt, to taste

For the garnish

* 1 small onion, cut into 8 wedges
* 4 tbsp olive oil
* salt and pepper, to taste

6. To make the parsley dressing, blend all the ingredients except the oils together in a blender until well blended. While continuing to blend, add the oils gradually. Check the seasoning.

7. To make the chickpea masabacha, drain and rinse the soaked chickpeas well, then place them in a pan with twice their volume of water. Simmer for 1 hour, skimming off any foam from time to time.

8. Add the baking soda, garlic and chile, and cook for another 30 minutes–1 hour, continuing to skim. The chickpeas need to be soft but not overcooked and mushy. Strain but reserve ½ cup of the cooking liquid along with the garlic and the chile. Chop the chile roughly.

9. Place the chickpeas in a saucepan with the garlic, chile, reserved cooking liquid and Jerusalem Spice Mix. Bring to a simmer and roughly mush with a fork, then add the herbs, lemon juice and the spoonful of dressing. Check for seasoning (it needs to be sour, a bit hot and spicy), adding salt to taste, and set aside. This also goes brilliantly simply with yogurt and some Harissa (see p.27).

10. Preheat your grill to its highest setting. Meanwhile, place the octopus steaks or chopped octopus and onion wedges on a baking sheet, season with the olive oil, salt and pepper and bring to room temperature. Grill for 2–3 minutes on each side until nice and golden brown (the onion should be a bit charred), then remove from the oven and dress with the rest of the parsley dressing.

11. To serve, divide the Baba Ganoush between 6 serving plates and top up with a couple of spoonfuls of masabacha. Place 3 confit cherry tomatoes on each plate, divide the octopus and onions between the plates and, finally, garnish with the parsley dressing.

The parsley dressing is excellent with grilled fish and seafood.

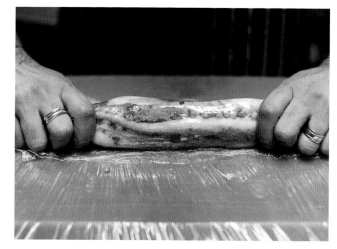

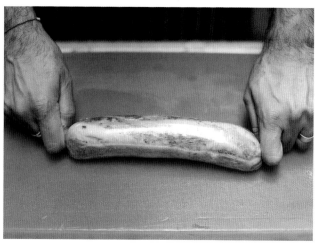

Mussels hamusta

Serves 4

This is a take on a favorite soup that my grandma used to make every Friday for lunch. The original version, called kubeh hamusta *(*hamusta *means "sour" in Kurdish), is a tangy soup with lots of greens and lemon, cooked with semolina dumplings filled with cow's neck confit meat. This sour soup is the most vivid memory I have of her; it was the last thing I ate before she died. I was pretty young when that happened, so I don't remember much about her, except that she really loved her sour flavors. Being a fairly religious Jew, she would probably have killed me if she knew I was adding seafood to her soup.*

---

1. This hamusta stock has a very fragrant, intense flavor and you can use this same method to push to the forefront any ingredients or flavorings you choose by blending them and then adding to vegetable, chicken or any other stock. To make the hamusta stock, place all the ingredients except the stock or water in a blender or food processor and blitz for 2–3 minutes until you have a smooth paste.

2. Pour the stock or water into a large pan, add the paste and bring to a boil. Reduce the heat and simmer until reduced to one-third. Strain through a fine sieve and set aside.

3. Heat a large, wide, shallow pan over a high heat (or 2 of your largest pans if you don't have one big enough), add the cleaned mussels (or clams) and leave them for 1–2 minutes to dry out a little (some will open and drain more liquid out, which is good). Add your favorite anise-flavored spirit (mine is arak; no doubt) and let it evaporate or be brave: set it alight and flambé it out. Cook for another 1–2 minutes, when most of your mussels will have opened up.

4. Add the hamusta stock, bring to a boil and cook for 3–4 minutes until the rest of the mussels have opened. If some are broken or have failed to open, discard them.

5. Add the fennel, zucchini shavings and celery and cook for 3–4 minutes more. By now, your liquid should have been reduced by half, but if that hasn't yet happened, give it another 2–3 minutes.

6. Add the Swiss chard leaves and stew (if using) and the butter, then shake the pan to get a nice emulsified sauce. Add the lemon juice, herbs and salt and pepper. Taste to see if you're happy with the flavor — you can add a bit more lemon juice if you want it extra sour.

* 3⅓ lbs live mussels (or clams) (if using mussels, make sure you scrub them well and debeard them, discarding any damaged ones)
* ½ cup anise-flavored spirit, such as arak, Pernod or ouzo
* 1 fennel bulb, thinly sliced (a mandoline will make your life easy here, but watch your fingers!)
* 1 zucchini, shaved all the way with a vegetable peeler
* 2 celery ribs, peeled with a peeler (to remove those annoying strings), then thinly sliced on the diagonal
* 4 Swiss chard leaves (green parts only), washed and roughly chopped
* 3 tbsp Swiss Chard Stew (see p.128), optional
* ½ cup butter, cut into cubes
* 4 tbsp freshly squeezed lemon juice, plus extra to taste
* generous handful of chopped parsley
* generous handful of chopped cilantro
* salt and pepper, to taste

Variations

You can add a little cooked pearl barley, chickpeas or even beans if you want the dish to be a bit more substantial, but as always, I love to eat it with a lot of Challah (see p.238) or Kubaneh Bread (see p.230) to dip in the sauce.

For the hamusta stock

* 1 onion, cut into quarters
* 4 garlic cloves, peeled
* 1 fennel bulb, cut into quarters
* 4 celery ribs, roughly chopped
* 2 tbsp Swiss Chard Stew (see p.128) or 3 Swiss chard leaves (green parts only), washed
* 1 tsp toasted cumin seeds
* 1 tsp toasted coriander seeds
* 6⅓ cups vegetable stock (see p.123 for homemade) or water

- * 4 tbsp canola oil
- * 1–3 red chiles, sliced (depending on how hot you like it)
- * 5 red peppers, cored, seeded and cut into ⅜-inch fingers
- * 5 garlic cloves, sliced
- * 1 tbsp sweet paprika
- * 1 tsp toasted and ground cumin seeds
- * 1 tsp Hawaij Spice Mix (see p.20), optional
- * 5 tbsp anise-flavored spirit, such as arak, Pernod or ouzo (optional)
- * ½ cup water
- * 1 tbsp Harissa (see p.27)
- * 14.5oz can good-quality chopped tomatoes
- * pinch of sugar
- * 4 cod fillets, ⅓ lb each, skinned
- * salt, to taste
- * 1 large bunch of cilantro, chopped
- * squeeze of lemon juice

Cod chraymeh

Serves 4

The name of this North African fish stew is derived from the word chraimee, *which in slang means "bastard," and alludes to the way of preparing and eating this dish — fast and hot, almost "stealing" it by snatching it up quickly with a piece of bread. Basically a great and fast way to cook a nice piece of fat fish for fortifying the laborers of Libya, Algeria, Tunisia and Morocco on their lunch breaks. Chraymeh found its way into the Jewish kitchen as a quick fish dish for just before the Sabbath enters, since it is the custom on a Friday always to have a fish course before the meat. It has now been taken into the heart of almost every Israeli household as the official Friday night fish dish, and even Ashkenazi — originally Eastern European — households cook it with joy.*

In this recipe I use fresh red peppers and canned tomatoes because I like mine chunky — alternatively you can use tomato purée and some water if you prefer a smooth texture. Although I use cod here, any white flaky fish will do, such as hake or halibut, and feel free to turn it into a seafood festival by adding clams, mussels, shrimp and even scallops, all poached quickly in the fragrant red stew.

---

1. Heat a large saucepan or a wide, shallow pan over a medium heat, add the oil, chiles and peppers and sauté for 15 minutes, stirring occasionally. Add the garlic and half the dry spices and cook for another 5 minutes.

2. Add the anise-flavored spirit (if using) and crank the heat up to allow the alcohol to vaporize, then add the water and Harissa and stir for a while.

3. Next add the tomatoes and sugar, then let the stew simmer for 10–15 minutes before adding the rest of the ingredients.

4. Season the cod fillets with salt, then gently slide them into the stew. (If you're using shellfish (mussels, clams, scallops etc), now is a good time to add them. Add half the cilantro and simmer for another 5 minutes.

5. Add the squeeze of lemon juice, give the stew a good shake and check for salt, then turn the heat off and let it rest for 5 minutes before you serve, topped with the rest of the cilantro. In my house, we put the pan straight on the table and everyone helps themselves. Grab a fork in one hand and a piece of bread in the other.

Hake with deep-fried cauliflower

Serves 4

This dish was created for one of our first tasting menus at the restaurant. It was the first time I'd deep-fried a cauliflower on British soil. It's an easy dish to make if you've mastered the first two chapters covering the basics and mezze. I use hake because it's firm yet flaky and the skin tastes really good when it's crispy. In the restaurant we use a plancha grill to cook the fish, but a nonstick pan will do the trick just as well. You can use any other flaky white fish (try red snapper or halibut) and feel free to add some scallops, shrimp or mussels to the pan — they all work brilliantly.

---

1. Heat the oil for deep-frying in a deep saucepan to 340–350°F (see p.55). Deep-fry the cauliflower steaks, one by one, until they're a golden brown color, then remove and drain on paper towels. Season to taste with salt, the cumin and half the lemon juice. Whenever deep-frying, it's important to season the ingredients straight as they come out of the oil, as they will then absorb the seasoning so much better and it also helps to get rid of any excess oil.

2. While you're in the process of deep-frying, heat a large nonstick pan until very hot. Season the fish with salt and pepper. I also like to season the skin with a bit of salt so that it will then crisp up really well. Add the olive oil with the extra spoonful of canola or vegetable oil (which helps the olive oil to reach a high temperature without burning), then place the fish in the pan, skin-side down, and press it lightly so that it doesn't curl upward. This will make sure that your skin will be evenly crisp and golden (you can give the pan a small shake 10 seconds after the fish goes in to avoid it sticking to the base). After 2 minutes, reduce the heat to medium and continue to sear for 2–3 minutes — we're looking for that golden brown halo with the flesh starting to turn white. Now flip the fish, and if your fillets are thicker than ¾ inch, then cook them for an extra minute before the next step.

3. Turn off the heat and add the rest of the lemon juice to the pan. It will sizzle and caramelize, and will make you and the fish very happy.

4. To serve, divide the Velvet Tomatoes among 4 serving plates, add the White Tahini Sauce around it (to go for the pro look, use a plastic squeezy bottle), then drizzle the Tapenade over the sauce. Place the cauliflower on the tomatoes and the fish on the cauliflower, then drizzle with the Schug.

* 4¼ cups canola or vegetable oil, for deep-frying, plus 1 tbsp
* 1 cauliflower, cut into 4 "steaks" 1 inch thick (trim the cauliflower of any leaves, then cut lengthwise into steaks)
* salt, to taste
* 1 tsp toasted and ground cumin seeds
* ¼ cup freshly squeezed lemon juice
* 4 hake fillets, skin on, about ⅓ lb each (ask your fishmonger to prep them — they'll be happy to)
* black pepper, to taste
* 2 tbsp olive oil
* ½ cup Velvet Tomatoes (see p.30)
* ½ cup White Tahini Sauce (see p.28)
* 8 tsp Tapenade (see p.35)
* 8 tsp Schug (see p.34)

For the garnish

* 4 tsp Cured Lemon Paste
  (see p.25)
* 4 tsp Harissa (see p.27)
* handful of cilantro/micro
  leaves
* 4 green chiles, flame-grilled
* salt, to taste
* drizzle of olive oil (optional)
* lemon wedges, to serve

For the fennel salad

* 1 orange
* 1 grapefruit
* 1 fennel bulb, thinly sliced
* 10 black Moroccan olives, pitted and chopped (Greek Thassos olives are also good)
* 1 tbsp Harissa (see p.27)
* 1 tbsp olive oil
* salt, to taste

For the sardines

* handful of chopped parsley
* handful of chopped cilantro
* 1 red onion, finely diced
* 2 garlic cloves, thinly sliced
* 2 tbsp dried bread crumbs
* handful of rolling pin–bashed toasted slivered almonds (just put them in a bag and bash, bash, bash!)
* 2 tbsp Cured Lemon Paste (see p.25)
* 1 tsp Harissa (see p.27)
* 2 tbsp olive oil
* salt, to taste
* 8 large sardines, anchovies or mackerel, scaled, gutted, butterflied and deboned (ask your fishmonger to help — they'll be happy to)
* 4 tbsp all-purpose flour
* ½ cup canola oil

Mz'uz'in

"Married" sardines with fennel, citrus & harissa
Serves 4

The meaning of the word mz'uz'in *in Moroccan is "coupled" or "married," and who doesn't like a good wedding? You take the bride and groom, stuff them with lots of herbs, Harissa, Cured Lemon Paste and almonds, invite some guests — fennel, grapefruit, orange and olives — and bring along a band of flame-grilled chiles and you've got yourself a great party. You'll never look at sardines the same way.*

———

1. To make the fennel salad, cut off the top and bottom of the orange and grapefruit with a serrated knife. Sit the fruit on the chopping board and cut away the rind and white pith from the top to the bottom, turning the fruit around until only the flesh is left. Then cut between the membranes to extract the beautiful, pith-free segments. Squeeze about 4 tablespoons of the juice from the leftover core and strain.
2. Place the citrus segments and juice with the rest of the ingredients in a bowl, season with salt and mix gently. This salad is also great as a mezze.
3. For the sardines, combine the herbs, onion, garlic, bread crumbs, almonds, Cured Lemon Paste, Harissa, olive oil and some salt in a bowl to make the filling.
4. Make sure your butterflied sardine fillets are free of all bones and scales, then lay 4 of them out flat, flesh-side up, and divide the filling between them. Then cover with the rest of the butterflied fillets, flesh-side down. Place the flour on a tray and dust the stuffed sardines with it on both sides.
5. Heat a large nonstick skillet to a medium heat and add the canola oil. When the oil is hot, gently place your sardines in the pan (if your pan is not big enough for one batch of 4, use less oil and cook them in 2 batches — the oil should submerge only half the sardine). You can also go for the alternative option of barbecuing or grilling them, which is a bit easier and uses slightly less oil; just skip the flouring stage and make sure you brush them lightly with oil before cooking on a hot barbecue or on a baking sheet under a hot grill. Fry or grill the sardines for 2–3 minutes, then flip them over and cook for another 2–3 minutes. Remove the fried sardines from the oil and pat dry with paper towels before seasoning with salt, or just season the grilled sardines with salt.
6. To serve, smear the edges of your serving plates with the Cured Lemon Paste and Harissa, and place the fennel salad and then the sardines on top. Pile the cilantro/micro leaves and chiles on the side, then season with salt and drizzle with olive oil (if using). Serve with lemon wedges.

For the Middle Eastern chimichurri

* handful of chopped watercress
* handful of chopped parsley
* 2 handfuls of chopped cilantro
* handful of chopped fresh oregano
* 1 small red onion, diced
* 1 garlic clove, finely grated
* ½ unwaxed lemon, first sliced into rounds, then seeded and cut into ¼-inch cubes, including the rind
* 1 tsp sweet paprika
* ½ tsp toasted and ground cumin seeds
* ½ tsp crushed red pepper flakes
* ½ tsp chile powder or hot paprika
* ½ cup canola oil
* ½ cup olive oil
* 1½ tbsp freshly squeezed lemon juice
* 1½ tbsp white wine vinegar
* salt, to taste

For the harissa mash

* 1 recipe of Creamy Mash (see p.186)
* 1 heaping tbsp Harissa (see p.27)

→ Ingredients and recipe continued on next page

Ribeye with harissa mash & Middle Eastern chimichurri

Serves 4

Steak dishes are the hardest to create for a restaurant, which I should qualify by saying — good, interesting, different and original steak dishes. Let's face it, when you crave a great steak, all you care about is the quality of the meat and that it's cooked the way you like it. But for me that's not enough — well, sometimes it is if it's just for me personally, as I'm easy to please. However, for my guests and for you I have to go the extra mile.

The inspiration for the chimichurri came from a blasphemous version I made for my Argentinian friend Lucas, a sous chef at Machneyuda who balked at the addition of cilantro. This version is packed with cilantro, cumin and paprika. The braised sweetheart (also known as pointed or hispi) cabbage is a great British ingredient to which I've added a Middle Eastern twist. And the harissa mash serves to tie the whole thing together.

———

1. Start with the chimichurri, as it needs to sit for a good couple of hours. Simply mix all the ingredients together in a bowl — you can do this a day ahead and keep it in the fridge, covered tightly with plastic wrap. It will, however, last for up to a week in a sterilized airtight container (see p.24). You can also use it with any grilled fish, meat or chicken, or try a touch of it with fresh oysters.

2. For the harissa mash, once your Creamy Mash is good to go, simply fold through the spoonful of Harissa.

3. For the braised sweetheart cabbage, preheat your oven to 400°F and place the cabbage quarters in a baking sheet deep enough to hold them. Season with salt, the cumin, sugar, crushed red pepper flakes and coriander seeds, then add the anise-flavored spirit to the baking sheet and a bacon or pancetta half strip and a pat of butter to each cabbage quarter.

4. Cover with foil and bake for 15 minutes. Remove from the oven and let stand, covered, for 10 minutes. Lift off the foil and heat your grill to its highest setting, or fire up the barbecue if it's a nice sunny day, and grill for 5–7 minutes. It's fine if it's a bit scorched — that will only add to the flavor! You can do the grilling bit while you're cooking your steaks so that they'll be ready at the same time for you to serve.

5. For the steaks, the star turn, there are two ways to go here: cooking over a powerful gas or charcoal barbecue (but don't grill in the oven) or pan-searing. Both work well, so I'll explain both.

To barbecue, clarify your butter by simply melting it in the microwave or gently heating in a pan on the burner, then pouring off the clear fat and discarding the milk solids. Mix with the oils and let your steaks temper in the mixture for 10 minutes.

Take the steaks out, pat dry slightly with paper towels and season with salt and pepper. Sear the steaks at a 45-degree angle to the rungs of the barbecue rack for 90 seconds, then rotate 90 degrees and sear for another 90 seconds — this will give you that cool pro-chef crisscross effect. Flip the steaks and repeat the process on the other side, then leave them to rest on a tray or wooden board for 5 minutes while you assemble up the other elements.

To pan-fry, heat 2 of your largest, heaviest skillets for a good 3–4 minutes over a maximum heat — if you have an extractor fan, now would be a good time to turn it on to full power, as it's going to get a bit smoky. Season your steaks with salt and pepper, add the oils to the pans and place the steaks in them gently. Sear for 2½ minutes, then flip and add the butter. Now comes my favorite part, the *arrosage* or "watering" in French, like you'd water a lawn — in other words basting. Tilt the pan and, using a spoon, "water" your steak constantly with the butter for 2 minutes. This is a highly pleasurable action for every chef and cook out there — I'm sure once you've tried it, you'll understand me, as there's something very loving and caring about it, almost as though you're babysitting your steak. Take the steaks out of the pans and leave them to rest as above.

6. To serve, divide the mash between the serving plates, add the cabbage and the steaks, sprinkling each one with some Maldon salt flakes (if using) and finishing with a fat, tasty spoonful of the chimichurri.

For the steaks

* ¼ cup butter
* 2 tbsp olive oil
* 2 tbsp canola oil
* 4 dry-aged ribeye steaks, ½ lb each, at room temperature
* salt and pepper
* Maldon salt flakes (optional)

For the braised sweetheart cabbage

* 1 sweetheart cabbage, outer layer of leaves discarded, then cut into quarters
* salt, to taste
* 1 tsp toasted and ground cumin seeds
* 1 tsp sugar
* pinch of crushed red pepper flakes
* 1 tsp toasted coriander seeds
* ¼ cup anise-flavored spirit, such as arak, Pernod or ouzo
* 2 streaky bacon or pancetta slices, cut in half
* 3½ tbsp butter

FOR THOSE
WHO WANT TO
KICK BACK

———————

A selection of our signature cocktails

A LIFE IN THE MIX
by Marco Torre

I guess it was back in 2000 that I began to take bartending seriously. At the outset, it was the fun, social aspect of the job that appealed to me. I loved the interaction with colleagues and guests, the frenetic environment, and I still get a kick from all that, but I hadn't yet really appreciated the craft involved. The first cocktail bar I worked in was AKA in London's Covent Garden, which was, of course, next to The End, both run by Layo and Zoe Paskin. It was the first DJ bar in the UK, stocking a wide selection of spirits and sporting a strong cocktail list. I was fortunate to work with some very skilled bartenders who had all trained under the renowned Dick Bradsell and had come from some of the top bars in London at the time, such as the Met Bar and the Match Bar. The standard was high and I had to work hard and fast to keep up with those mixologists. AKA was open and slamming five nights a week, and ran nonstop through the weekends. It was the perfect place for a 23-year-old Italian boy without a clear idea of his future and yet eager to learn a new profession. I suddenly realized... bartending wasn't just about making vodka and tonic or tequila shots. There was an art and a whole world behind it: the history of cocktails and spirits, the craft of tending a bar, the science involved in making drinks. I started developing a deep interest in mixing flavors and learning what is actually in any given bottle of booze—the long journey that makes a plant into a great drink.

Since the Negroni is my ultimate choice of desert island cocktail, its ingredients are always in my cabinet; it's probably my Italian background that has given me a passion for all vermouths and bitters. I have always been fascinated by classic cocktails and their simplicity, and I love to create modern variations of those timeless drinks. The way I see cocktails are like most things I admire in life — there is nothing more exciting than striving for perfection in creating and mixing a drink. It's addictive.

At The Palomar, I have the opportunity to run a small bar alongside a dedicated and skilled kitchen. All of our bartenders are fully involved in the development of the cocktail list: it is creative teamwork, as with every other aspect of the restaurant. We have a 10-strong cocktail list that changes regularly, where we offer a variety of key spirit choices to satisfy most palates, but we also like to maintain a good balance between aperitifs and after-dinner drinks. Here are some of our greatest hits.

DRUNKEN BOTANIST

A great aperitif made with all the bartender's favorite ingredients! We created this by giving a twist to the Cardinale cocktail, which is basically a drier version of a Negroni. When we devised the Drunken Botanist, we didn't compromise through concern about whether or not the customers would like it, but instead focused on coming up with something authentic that we truly wanted to drink. Early on in the days of my bartending I thought Campari was a really bitter drink, but now with a few years on the clock I find it very sweet. Our palates evolve as we grow up, and this is very definitely a grown-up drink.

For the saline

* 5 parts water
* 1 part salt

Ingredients

* 2 tbsp gin
* 4 tsp Campari
* 1 tbsp dry vermouth (ideally Dolin)
* 1 tsp Fernet Branca
* ½ tsp green Chartreuse
* 1 dash Maraschino
* orange peel twist, to garnish

1. To make the saline, heat the water and salt together in a saucepan, stirring, until the salt has dissolved, then leave to cool. Store in a sterilized dropper bottle (see p.24) in a cool, dark place. It will keep for up to 1 month.

2. Stir all the cocktail ingredients together in a mixing glass and add 1 drop of saline. Strain into a chilled coupette. Garnish with a twist of orange peel.

**For the honey and
ginger syrup**

* 1½ parts runny honey
* 1 part fresh ginger juice

Ingredients

* ¼ cup gin
* 4 tsp freshly squeezed
  lemon juice
* ¼ tsp orange curaçao
* 2 dashes orange bitters
* ice cubes
* orange peel twist,
  to garnish

BUMBLEBEE

I have always been fascinated by honey — where it
comes from and how it's produced — and I love that it
can be used as a healthy alkaline sweetener. I wanted
to make a cocktail without refined sugar; sweetness is
a key component in both food and drinks, but how to
get away from the refined stuff? I drew inspiration from
an old Prohibition cocktail called a Bee's Knees, which
was a mix of gin, honey and lemon juice. From there
on it was straightforward: I made a syrup of honey and
ginger juice and combined it with the lemon juice, gin
and curaçao, a liqueur made from the dried peel
of bitter oranges. (See photograph on p.181.)

1. To make the honey and ginger syrup, blend the honey and ginger juice until
smooth. Pour into a sterilized airtight bottle (see p.24), seal and chill in the
fridge. It will keep for up to 2 weeks.
2. Put all the cocktail ingredients into a cocktail shaker and add 4 tsp Honey
and Ginger Syrup. Shake and serve over ice in a rocks glass. Garnish with a curl
of orange peel.

For the mint syrup

* 2 parts just-boiled water
* 1 part fresh mint leaves
* 1 part granulated sugar

Ingredients

* 3 tbsp vodka
* 4 tsp freshly squeezed lemon juice
* 2 tsp grappa alla liquirizia
* ½ tsp green Chartreuse
* Angostura bitters, in a spray bottle or atomizer, to garnish

INTO THE WILD

This drink was created by one of our team, Giuseppe, and is an excellent palate cleanser that pairs well with our fresh and spicier food. The licorice makes it a great digestif due to its soothing properties.

1. To make the mint syrup, brew a strong mint tea with the just-boiled water and mint leaves. Mix 1 part hot mint tea with 1 part granulated sugar until the sugar has dissolved, then filter through a muslin. Pour into a sterilized airtight bottle (see p.24), seal and chill in the fridge. It will keep for up to 1 week.
2. Put all the cocktail ingredients into a cocktail shaker and add 1 tbsp of mint syrup. Shake and double strain into a Nick & Nora glass. Garnish with 2 sprays of Angostura bitters.

BISHBASH POSH WASH

This was created by another of our team, John, to mimic the torta de aceite — a traditional Spanish sweet, crisp, flaky biscuit flavored with anise and fennel. The word bishbash is Moroccan for fennel, while "wash" is the method of infusing the vodka. Basically, this is a spin on the great vodka martini, with notes of fennel, caraway and anise. (See photograph on p.4.)

1. To make the butter and olive oil–washed vodka, melt the butter with the oil in a saucepan and mix together, then add the vodka and stir well.
2. Pour the mixture into a strong, sealable plastic food bag and heat in a water bath of warm water, at 140°F for about 20 minutes.
3. Remove the bag from the warm water and leave to rest for a few minutes, then place the bag in the freezer for several hours until the butter and oil become solid.
4. Remove the bag from the freezer and filter the vodka through muslin, discarding the solids. Pour into a sterilized airtight bottle (see p.24), seal and chill in the fridge. It will keep in the freezer for up to 1 month.
5. Add all the cocktail ingredients together in a mixing glass and stir in 4 tbsp of the butter and olive oil–washed vodka. Pour into a Nick & Nora glass. Garnish with the tuile.

For the butter and olive oil–washed vodka

* ½ cup clarified unsalted butter
* 1¼ cups olive oil
* 3 cups of vodka

Ingredients

* 1 tsp kümmel liqueur
* ½ tsp dry vermouth, (ideally Dolin)
* ¼ tsp arak
* 1 drop Saline (see Drunken Botanist)
* Tuile (substitute the hazelnuts for fennel seeds, see p.200), to garnish

LION'S MILK

They call arak the lion's drink, hence the name of this cocktail. Arak is drunk everywhere in the Middle East — there are pop-up bars selling it around the markets, and one of the most popular ways to drink it in Israel is with grapefruit juice. We wanted to go a little more radical... (See photograph on p.227.)

1. To make the almond milk, soak the slivered almonds in the 2⅔ cups water for 12 hours. Pour into a blender with the sugar and blend until smooth, then filter through muslin. Pour into a sterilized airtight bottle (see p.24), seal and chill in the fridge. It will keep for up to 1 week.
2. Bruise the mint leaves and add to a rocks glass. Build the remaining cocktail ingredients over ice and top up with ¼ cup of the almond milk and stir. Garnish with a mint sprig.

For the almond milk

* 2 cups slivered almonds
* 2⅔ cups water
* 1 cup granulated sugar

Ingredients

* 8 fresh mint leaves, plus 1 sprig of mint to garnish
* ice cubes
* 5 tsp arak
* 2 dashes orange bitters

For the coconut foam

* 1 tbsp sugar syrup, made with 2 parts granulated sugar to 1 part water (see method)
* ¾ cup water
* ¾ cup coconut milk
* ½ tbsp egg white powder
* ½ tsp of gelatin

Ingredients

* 5 tsp Wray & Nephew White Overproof Rum
* 5 tsp freshly squeezed lime juice
* 4 tsp Taylor's Velvet Falernum
* 24 tsp Aperol
* 2 dashes orange bitters

DAIQUIRI NUCLEARE

In the same way that chefs reinterpret classics, bartenders invent spins on cocktails or other bartenders' drinks. Here I have created a new take on the Nuclear Daiquiri from the late Gregor de Gruyther, bartender extraordinaire, who often came to AKA after his shifts at the LAB bar in Soho where he worked.

This is a party drink with a great kick. I have swapped the green Chartreuse for the Italian aperitif Aperol. To complement the tropical notes of its main player Wray & Nephew rum, I have garnished it with a coconut foam, which both looks and tastes fantastic.

1. To make the sugar syrup for the coconut foam, heat the granulated sugar and water together in a saucepan, stirring, until the sugar has dissolved, then leave to cool. Store in a sterilized airtight bottle (see p.24) in a cool, dark place. It will keep for up to 1 month.

2. To make the coconut foam, warm all the remaining ingredients except the gelatin in a saucepan over a medium heat for a few minutes, mixing with a whisk. Add the gelatin to the pan and keep whisking until it has completely dissolved.

3. Put the mixture into a whipping siphon and charge according to the manufacturer's instructions. Chill in the fridge.

4. To make the cocktail, put all the cocktail ingredients into a cocktail shaker, shake and double strain into a small chilled coupette. Garnish with the coconut foam.

For the sumac tincture

* 1 part sumac
* 1 part vodka

Ingredients

* ice cubes
* 2 tbsp freshly squeezed lemon juice
* 5 tsp gomme syrup
* lemon peel twist and a mint sprig, to garnish

SUMAC-ADE

Our head bartender, John, and I have been playing with Middle Eastern flavors since The Palomar opened. Although we've created an alcoholic cocktail with sumac, this almost virgin Sumac-ade really stands out. It's a take on the classic British fresh lemonade, but we've added some sumac tincture, which contributes tartness and shades of red berry fruit. The tincture is made with a high-alcohol neutral spirit and yet the amount of alcohol in the finished drink is really low.

1. To make the sumac tincture, mix the sumac into the neutral spirit or vodka and leave to infuse for 48 hours. Filter through a muslin and store in a sterilized dropper bottle (see p.24) in a cool, dark place. It will keep for up to 1 year.

2. Build the cocktail ingredients over ice cubes in a highball glass and stir in ¼ tsp of the sumac tincture. Garnish with a lemon twist and a mint sprig.

For the black pepper tincture

* 2 parts ground black pepper
* 1 part vodka

Ingredients

* ¼ cup Rittenhouse 100 Proof rye whiskey
* 2 tsp Pedro Ximénez sherry, ideally Lustau San Emilio
* 2 tsp dry Curaçao, ideally Pierre Ferrand
* 1 tsp Fernet Branca
* orange peel twist, to garnish

BLACK SPICE

I created this drink based on one of my favorite classic cocktails, the Rye Sweet Manhattan. I used a bold and spicy rye whiskey but combined it with sweet sherry instead of the traditional vermouth and Fernet Branca, an Italian bitter, in place of Angostura bitters. It turned out to be an excellent digestif, deceptively simple in its ingredients yet satisfyingly complex in its flavor profile.

1. To make the black pepper tincture, mix the ground black pepper into the neutral spirit or vodka and leave to infuse for 48 hours. Filter through muslin (or an empty teabag) and store in a sterilized dropper bottle (see p.24) in a cool, dark place. It will keep for up to 1 year. The yield will be very low but with a wonderful concentration of flavor.

2. Add all the cocktail ingredients together in a mixing glass and stir in 1 drop of the black pepper tincture. Serve in a cocktail glass. Garnish with a curl of orange peel.

COCKTAILS
A (very) uncertain past
by Layo Paskin

It goes a little something like this… In the
18th century, the English, never shy of enjoying vast
quantities of beer and port, switched to spirits —
namely gin — to avoid a newly created beer tax.
The word "cocktail" has numerous stories of
origin. Our favorite features the disreputable
practice of gingering horses for market. Put
bluntly, this involved putting ginger in the horses'
backsides to "cock the tail."
The Americans added ginger to drinks which they
then swapped to bitters, and the word "cocktail"
appeared in 1803 in Vermont. Recipes began to
surface through the 19th and into the 20th century.
Here is our very modest 21st-century contribution
to the lexicon.

MODERN-DAY JERUSALEM COOKING
& THE ASHKENAZI/SEPHARDIC/MIZRAHI RIDDLE

by Tomer Amedi

Jerusalem is a huge melting pot. It is where I was born and raised — a city that has been occupied by almost every Empire in history, which mixes Jews from all over the world, Muslims and Christians. There are Ashkenazi Jews from Eastern Europe and Russia; Sephardi Jews originally from Spain and the Maghreb (North Africa); and my gang, the lesser-known Mizrahi (eastern) Jews, from Yemen to Turkey, Jordan to Lebanon, Syria to Iran.

Our journey starts with the mass exile of the Israelites from Judea in 70AD. Finding themselves scattered from Spain to Russia, from Germany to Yemen, they created new communities, assimilating within each region. The threads that continued to bind Jewish communities around the world were their religious customs, Jewish culture and food: special dishes cooked for holidays, the Sabbath, weddings and memorial days.

The Mizrahi gang has been settled in their region for the longest of the three tribes, with little movement over their 2,000-year history. They bonded with their indigenous communities, sharing folklore and ways of life, and in many respects have more in common with our Arab brothers than with Ashkenazi Jews.

In 1492 the Spanish Inquisition ordered the expulsion of all Jews from Spain. This spread the Sephardic Jews across Morocco, Tunisia, France and Italy, again adapting and absorbing elements of new cultures and cuisines. From the late 19th century the Ashkenazi Jews began to return to Israel. This culminated in a huge influx from Europe following World War II, when Jews finally had a home to return to after 2,000 years of exile.

I'm the luckiest chef alive. Unwittingly, effortlessly, I have been exposed to a wealth of cuisines — in effect traveling without moving. With The Palomar, the journey continues.

The Kitchen Bar at Machneyuda

Hanger Steak & latkes

Serves 4

Aside from ribeye, this is my favorite cut of beef. It comes from the diaphragm area of the animal and has a strong taste: tender but with fibers that give it a lot of character, kind of like the hero in a Tarantino movie. This cut needs quick and hot treatment, and I would never have it cooked beyond medium, so if you belong to the medium-to-well-done club, feel free to replace it with a filet or a ribeye steak. In the restaurant we cook it in the fierce and hot Josper charcoal oven, but a heavy-bottomed cast-iron skillet heated until smoking hot will do the trick if you're indoors. If you're in barbecuing mode outside, get the barbecue really hot first.

---

1. First let's temper the meat, which needs to be done 30 minutes before cooking. Melt the butter in a small saucepan or in the microwave, then steep your steaks in it, leaving it somewhere warm enough that the butter will stay melted. I've found this is the best way to temper meat with a low fat content.

2. Preheat your oven to 400°F. Place the marrow bones in a roasting pan and roast for 20–25 minutes. You can then turn the oven off and leave them inside to keep hot until you serve.

3. To make the latkes, squeeze the grated potatoes to get rid of any liquid (it's best to do this in a sieve over the sink) and place in a mixing bowl. Add the flour, egg and herbs and season to taste with salt and pepper. Shape into 4 large, thin patties (make sure you don't make them too thick, otherwise they will remain raw in the middle).

4. Fry the latkes in the butter and oil in a large nonstick skillet over a medium heat until they are golden brown on both sides. Remove from the pan and place on paper towels to drain.

5. Blanch the broccolini in a large pot of salted boiling water for a minute and then chuck into iced water. Drain and set aside.

6. Heat a heavy-bottomed cast iron griddle until it smokes. Take the onglet out of the butter and pat with paper towels to blot off any excess butter. Season with salt and pepper, then sear it for 2 minutes on each side. Remove the onglet from the pan to rest on a board. In the same pan, sear the broccolini for 30 seconds (the pan will be so hot they will cook off the heat) and give them a squeeze of lemon juice and some salt. Next, fry 4 eggs sunny side up in a large nonstick skillet with the butter you've got left from the tempering, then season with salt and pepper.

7. To serve, divide the latkes and bone marrow among 4 serving plates, or wooden boards if you want to do it Palomar style. Place the broccolini and then the steaks on the plates, top with the eggs and season with salt and pepper.

* ¼ cup butter
* 4 trimmed hanger steaks, ⅓ lb each
* 4 marrow bones, halved horizontally (ask your butcher, who'll be delighted to do this for you)
* ½ lb broccolini, trimmed
* salt and pepper, to taste
* squeeze of lemon juice
* 4 eggs

For the latkes
* 3 potatoes, peeled and grated, about 1⅓ lb
* 1 tbsp all-purpose flour
* 1 egg, lightly beaten
* 1 tsp chopped thyme
* 1 tsp chopped rosemary
* salt and pepper, to taste
* ¼ cup butter
* 2 tbsp canola oil

Shakshukit

Deconstructed kebab
Serves 4

This dish was born in the Machneyuda restaurant a couple of months after we opened. At that time, everybody in Jerusalem was serving kebabs with tahini and to go for the same boring concept seemed a bit uncool to us, so Papi worked his magic and came up with this deconstructed version. The toppings and the pita make it the ultimate mopping dish. I like the fact that you get a different flavor with each bite, but some people like to mix everything together before they eat it. Feel free to try both ways and decide for yourself. As always, it's important to get good-quality meat, but you won't ever regret the extra time and effort it takes to source it. By the way, you don't have to make all four toppings — I know it's a lot of work — but this is the way I like to eat it, so feel free to play and top in any way you like.

---

1. For the meat, place a large, shallow pan over a medium heat, add the oil and then the onion and sweat for 5 minutes. Add the pistachios and pine nuts and sauté for another 5 minutes, then add the garlic and sauté for another 3 minutes.

2. Add the ground meat in 3–4 batches, breaking up each batch with a wooden spoon and allowing it to cook for 3–4 minutes before you add the next batch so that you don't get lumps. You can increase the heat to high now, but just make sure you continue to stir.

3. After 10–15 minutes, add the rest of the ingredients and season to taste with salt and pepper. Cook over a medium heat for another 5 minutes so that all the flavors combine well.

4. Meanwhile, make the tahigurt. Mix all the tahigurt ingredients together in a bowl and divide among 4 soup plates (or funky pans, if you have some).

5. Divide the meat among the 4 plates and layer with all the toppings.

For the meat

* ¼ cup olive oil
* 1 large onion, chopped
* ⅓ cup pistachio nuts
* ⅓ cup pine nuts
* 4 garlic cloves, chopped
* 1lb ground beef
* ½lb ground lamb
* 1 tsp sweet paprika
* 1 tsp toasted and ground cumin seeds
* 1 tsp ground turmeric
* 1 tsp Hawaij Spice Mix (see p.20) (you can replace with toasted and ground cumin seeds)
* 1 tbsp Harissa (see p.27)
* 1 tbsp Cured Lemon Paste (see p.25)
* salt and pepper, to taste

For the tahigurt

* 1 cup Greek yogurt
* 5 tbsp tahini
* salt, to taste
* squeeze of lemon juice

For the toppings

* 4 tsp Harissa (see p.27)
* 4 tsp Cured Lemon Paste (see p.25)
* 4 tsp Watercress Pesto (see p.31)
* 4 tsp Tapenade (see p.35)
* 4 tbsp tahini paste
* 4 tbsp natural yogurt
* 4 Pita Breads (see p.229), to serve

Oxtail stew Persian style

Serves 4

Let me tell you a little story about a chef called Eliezer from our Machneyuda restaurant in Jerusalem. Everything this guy cooks tastes as if a 90-year-old grandma made it; he is blessed with the Midas touch — boy, it's annoying! So this recipe comes from Eliezer, who in turn learned it from a lovely grandma called Mina. It's inspired by a Persian stew called khoresht sabzi (khoresht meaning "stew" and sabzi "greens"), though in this version we use all the greens (mostly herbs) at the beginning rather than adding them at the end. Together with the dried limes, they give this stew an amazing floral-herbal fragrance. You can use any kind of meat suitable for long braising, such as neck, shank, legs or short ribs, but my personal favorite is oxtail, as the bone and amount of fat is perfect for slow cooking, and the end result is so succulent you'll think you've died and gone to heaven.

---

1. Heat a large frying pot over a high heat, season the oxtail with salt and pepper and 1 tablespoon of the Persian Stew Spice Mix and give the meat a good rub. Add 1 tablespoon of the oil to the pot and, working in batches, sear the oxtail evenly on all sides until it's brown, then transfer to a tray and turn off the heat under the pot.

2. When the pot has cooled down slightly, add the rest of the oil, the onions, white stalks of the Swiss chard and celery and return to a medium heat. Season to taste with salt and pepper and the rest of the spice mix. Sauté for about 10 minutes until the onions are soft, then add the garlic and sauté for another 3 minutes.

3. Add to the pan all the roughly chopped herbs and celery leaves with half the Swiss chard greens, keeping the rest aside with the finely chopped herbs for adding at the end, and mix well. Turn the heat up, return the oxtail to the pot and cook until the greens have lost their liquid and their flavors have concentrated, which will take about 10 minutes, stirring occasionally.

4. Add the stock or water and pomegranate molasses and bring to a boil. Reduce the heat to a gentle simmer, then add the dried limes, cover and cook over a very low heat for 5 hours. Alternatively, transfer to a covered ovenproof dish and cook in an oven preheated to 275°F.

5. Remove the lid, strain off ¼ pint of the cooking liquid and set aside (for this, I use a ladle, a sieve and a jug that can hold the sieve securely, then you have no mess). Add the barley to the pot and continue to simmer for another hour with the lid off, stirring occasionally. The starch from the barley will help to thicken the stew, and the liquid will reduce without compromising the tenderness of the meat.

6. While step 5 is happening, glaze the turnips. Start by blanching them in a large saucepan of boiling water for 3 minutes (this will help get rid of the bitterness), then drain well. Heat half the butter in a large skillet and add the sugar and then the turnips. Once the sugar has dissolved, add the oxtail cooking liquid you've reserved and boil until almost all the liquid has reduced and the turnips have a

For the stew

* 2¼ lb–3lb oxtail (ask your butcher to cut it into sections between the vertebrae)
* salt and pepper, to taste
* 2½ tbsp Persian Stew Spice Mix (see p.20; you can use 1 tsp each ground turmeric and toasted and ground cumin seeds and coriander seeds instead, but do make the effort if you can — you have no idea how much flavor and kick it adds)
* 3 tbsp canola oil
* 2 onions, diced
* 1 bunch of Swiss chard, washed, white stalks diced, leafy greens parts chopped
* 4 celery ribs, sliced into ¾-inch chunks
* 4 garlic cloves, sliced
* 3 handfuls of chopped parsley, 2 roughly chopped, 1 finely chopped
* 2 handfuls of chopped cilantro, ditto
* handful of roughly chopped mint
* handful of roughly chopped dill
* handful of roughly chopped celery leaves
* 8½ cups vegetable stock (see p.123 for homemade) or water
* 4 tbsp pomegranate molasses
* 2 dried limes (prick a hole in them before adding)
* ¾ cup pearl barley
* ¼ cup butter, cut into cubes
* ½ cup freshly squeezed lemon juice

For the glazed baby turnips

* 1 bunch of baby turnips (about 8–10), washed and trimmed a bit — I like to leave a little of the green tops intact (if you can't get hold of baby ones, go for 2–3 regular turnips cut into 1¼-inch chunks)
* 3 tbsp butter
* 1 tbsp sugar
* salt and pepper, to taste

gorgeous color. Now add the rest of the butter and shake, shake, shake the pan until nicely glazed all over. Season to taste with salt and pepper and set aside.

7. By now your oxtail stew liquid should have reduced by more than half and become thicker and powerful in flavor. But if that hasn't happened yet, don't panic — just give it an extra 30 minutes on a gentle simmer. We want a concentrated thick jus. When you're there, add the butter, lemon juice and the rest of the greens and check for salt.

8. To serve, divide the stew between serving plates, or just place the pan in the middle of the table with a serving spoon and top with the glazed turnips.

_____ **Nooshe jan!**
Bon appétit in Farsi, literally translating as "may your soul be nourished."

→ **Ingredients and recipe
continued on next page**

Chicken two ways
with freekeh

Serves 4

This was one of the hardest dishes to crack when we opened The Palomar, involving lots of testing and experimenting to get it right. It's a great example of the importance of team collaboration, especially with our sous chefs, and being able to take feedback even when it's a bit painful: a very important lesson in life. We know chicken is difficult to elevate above the familiar and homely. Anyone can create a nice enough chicken dish, but to make it original is a whole different story. So the approach was to devise some surprising flavors and textures. We started with four ingredients we knew we wanted to use: chicken thighs, buttermilk, freekeh and the Jerusalem Spice Mix. Thomas, my heroic sous chef (catchphrase: "Chef, I've got the Josper on 1300°F — do you think it's hot enough?"), came up with the crispy buttermilk drumstick; I came up with the "stroganoffed" shawarma-like thigh; Assaf came up with the butternut squash and cranberry in the freekeh; and Zoe and Layo ate a lot of chicken until we got the perfect balance… It was a tough job, but someone had to do it. The end result is this recipe. The freekeh also goes well with meat such as lamb and can be served as a vegetarian side dish or even as a sort of risotto (see p.175). Needless to say you can tweak the vegetables, herbs and spices any way you like. If the drumstick looks like a bit too much work, feel free to double the number of thighs, but I personally wouldn't do without it — who doesn't like fried chicken?

As with many of the recipes in this book, the best way to tackle this is to start all the processes in parallel. It's not as hard as it first appears; it just takes a bit of focus and in an hour you'll be enjoying a delicious chicken dish. Start with the drumsticks and thighs, as they'll need to cool between steps.

1. For the southern fried chicken-style drumsticks, place the drumsticks in a saucepan and cover with water. Add the onion, thyme, some salt and 1 tablespoon of the Jerusalem Spice Mix and bring to a boil, then reduce the heat and simmer for 20–25 minutes.

2. Remove the drumsticks to a tray and leave them to cool. (You can use the leftover cooking liquid to make a quick soup, if you'd like.)

3. Heat the oil for deep-frying in a deep saucepan to 340–350°F. While that's heating up, add 1 tablespoon of the Jerusalem Spice Mix and some salt to the buttermilk in a bowl and mix well. Add the final tablespoon of Jerusalem Spice Mix and some salt to the flour in a separate bowl and mix well, too.

4. Dip the drumsticks in the seasoned flour, then the seasoned buttermilk. Repeat the dipping sequence once more, finishing with the flour.

5. Deep-fry, one at a time, for 5 minutes until golden brown and crispy. Remove from the oil to a tray lined with paper towels and season with salt. Using a sheet of paper towel to protect your fingers from the heat (careful!), pop the end of the drumstick off — it should come away easily. Set the drumsticks aside until you are ready to serve. Try to coincide this step with step 7 and when your freekeh is ready.

6. For the stroganoffed thighs, rub the thighs with half the Jerusalem Spice Mix and some salt and pepper, and let them to sit for a bit — ideally overnight in the fridge. Heat your grill, or your barbecue, to a high heat. Place the thighs on a baking sheet and cook close to the grill, or on the barbecue, for 3 minutes on each side. It's good if they scorch a bit, as it adds to the flavor — in the restaurant we cook them in the powerful Josper charcoal grill and they always catch a tiny bit. Remove from the oven or barbecue and leave to cool, then roughly chop.

7. Heat a pan to maximum heat, add the cream, the rest of the Spice Mix and the chopped thighs and cook, stirring, for 5–7 minutes until the cream has thickened. Add the chopped herbs and set aside.

8. For the freekeh, blanch the butternut squash cubes in a large saucepan of salted boiling water for 2 minutes, then take them out but leave the pan of water simmering on the burner for the broccolini.

9. Heat the prepared freekeh in a saucepan, add the butternut cubes and chopped cranberries, season to taste with salt and pepper and the lemon juice and keep warm until you're ready to serve.

10. Blanch the broccolini for the garnish in the pan of salted water for 2 minutes, then remove to a bowl and season to taste with salt, 1 tablespoon of the lemon juice and 2 tablespoons of the olive oil. Place the herb leaves in a bowl and season them in the same way.

11. Now let's bring it all together. Divide the freekeh between the serving plates, place a drumstick and the broccolini on top and garnish with the herb leaves. If you want to go for the wow factor, put the stroganoffed thighs into a little sauce boat and add them at the table, Palomar style.

For the freekeh

* ½ butternut squash, peeled, seeded and cut into ½-inch cubes
* salt
* 1 recipe of Basic Freekeh (see p.175)
* 2 tbsp roughly chopped dried cranberries
* pepper, to taste
* squeeze of lemon juice

For the garnish

* ½ lb trimmed broccolini
* salt, to taste
* 2 tbsp freshly squeezed lemon juice
* 4 tbsp olive oil
* handful of parsley leaves
* handful of mint leaves
* handful of cilantro leaves

Chicken thighs in green olive & tomato sauce

Serves 4

This dish was born while we were in Jerusalem shooting the photos for this book, when my parents invited the whole gang for a Friday night meal. Needless to say my mama was ecstatic. "What should I make? Will it be enough? I'll make three more salads! We need to make something extra special!" she exclaimed. As we chatted about what to make, I remembered a dish she used to prepare a lot when I was young: a simple side of tomatoes and green olives that I really, really liked. We decided to serve it for the gang as a braised lamb shoulder stew. The meal was very special, with lots of arak, lots of laughs and tons of excellent food. The recipe here is with chicken, but you can replace it with any meat, or you can serve it the original way as a vegetarian side dish. I really like it with some couscous, plain rice or freekeh.

---

1. Start by rubbing the chicken with 1 tablespoon each of the Baharat and Ras el Hanout Spice Mixes and some salt, then set aside while you start the sauce. (You can do this the day before, then cover and leave the chicken thighs or legs in the fridge overnight — they'll be even tastier.)

2. Heat a wide, shallow pan over a medium heat, add the oils and then the onions and sauté with a pinch of salt and the crushed red pepper flakes for about 10–15 minutes until the onions are nicely caramelized.

3. While the onions are frying, bring a medium-sized saucepan of water to a boil, add 1 tablespoon of the lemon juice and blanch the olives for 2 minutes. Drain and then repeat this process twice more. Drain for the final time and set them aside.

4. When the onions have caramelized, add the garlic and sauté for 2–3 more minutes. Meanwhile, heat up a large nonstick pan over a medium heat, add the thighs or legs, skin-side down, and let them crisp up as they slowly render their fat.

5. Add half the stock (or water) to the onions and garlic. Meanwhile, when the thighs are nice and crisp on the skin side, flip them and sear on the other side as well. Season with a touch of salt and pepper, remove from the pan and leave to rest.

6. Add the remaining stock to the pan and deglaze it with a wooden spoon, combining the residue from the pan with the onions, garlic and stock. This will add amazing flavor to your sauce. If you've gone for the vegetarian version, just add all the vegetable stock to the onions in step 5 and skip from there to step 7.

* 8 chicken thighs or 4 whole legs (thighs and drumsticks)
* 2 tbsp Baharat Spice Mix (see p.20)
* 2 tbsp Ras el Hanout Spice Mix (see p.18)
* salt
* 2 tbsp olive oil
* 1 tbsp canola oil
* 2 onions, thinly diced
* 1 tsp crushed red pepper flakes
* 3 tbsp freshly squeezed lemon juice
* 1 cup plain pitted green olives (my favorites are Manzanilla)
* 8 garlic cloves, sliced
* 4¼ cups chicken or vegetable stock (see p.123 for homemade), or water if you can't get any (but do make the effort here to make some stock, it really lifts this dish up)
* pepper, to taste
* 2 14.5oz cans very good-quality chopped tomatoes (get the Italian stuff — they know their tomatoes)
* 1 tsp sugar
* handful of chopped parsley
* handful of chopped cilantro

7. When the stock has reduced by half (i.e. when you're left with about 2¼ cups, add the tomatoes, blanched olives, sugar and the rest of the spice mixes. Bring to a boil and then simmer for 10 minutes.

8. Add the chicken and simmer for another 20 minutes over a low heat. I like to turn the heat off and let the dish rest for at least 30–45 minutes before I serve, which binds all the flavors amazingly. Garnish with the chopped herbs and serve.

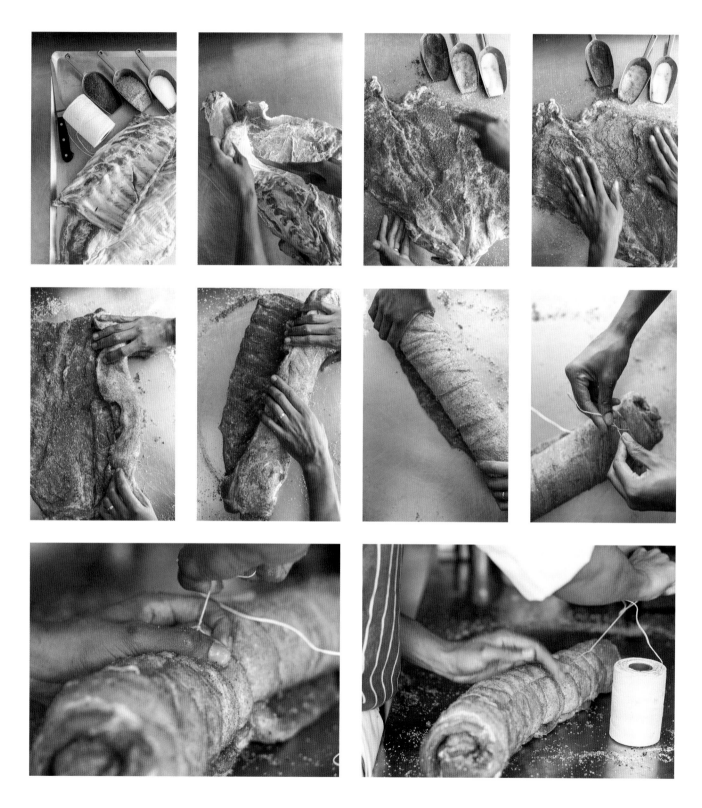

Pork belly with ras el hanout, dried fruits & Israeli couscous

Serves 4

This is the first dish I created exclusively for the restaurant. It embodies all the things that make The Palomar what it is: great local British ingredients (the pork), heritage and childhood memories (the Israeli couscous, the Moroccan flavors of my mama's cooking) and the modern chef's interpretation and techniques. Just like The Palomar, this dish encapsulates past and future, classic and modern — all wrapped up with a lot of love. In the restaurant we shape the belly into a roulade because I've found that's the best way to maximize the flavors and keep it moist and tender. It takes a bit of planning and preparation, so you'll need two days for this recipe, but it's a great one if you're hosting a big party. Israeli couscous goes excellently with all kinds of meat, stews and even seafood from the barbecue.

---

1. For the pork belly, if you're going with the roulade shape, start a day ahead. On a clean surface, season the belly with the sugar, 3 tablespoons of the Ras el Hanout Spice Mix and some salt and pepper, and rub in well all over. With the skin side down, roll the belly into a roulade and secure with butcher's twine (see photos on p.166–7). You'll need to make sure it's tied tightly, otherwise the belly will fall apart while cooking. Let it rest in the fridge for 4–5 hours (alternatively, leave it to rest overnight, in which case start 2 days ahead). If you're passing on the roulade, cut the belly into 2¾-inch cubes and then season and rest as for the roulade.

2. Place the dried fruits in a saucepan with the 2½ cups water and simmer for 20 minutes. Strain and keep both the cooking liquid and fruits. (This can also be done a day ahead.)

3. Heat a heavy-bottomed saucepan large enough to fit the roulade with plenty of room to spare (you'll need space for a lot of cooking liquid, but see step 4 if you don't have a pan big enough), add half the oil and sear the roulade on all sides (the sugar will burn a bit, but don't worry — just make sure you flip it on all sides every 2 minutes or so). Add all the vegetables and sear for another 3–4 minutes.

4. Add the poaching liquid, half the dried fruits, the orange (give it a nice squeeze before you add) and the rest of the Ras el Hanout, then cover with water. Bring to a boil, then reduce the heat to a very gentle simmer. Place a sheet of parchment paper on top and cover with a lid. Cook for 4 hours, checking from time to time that the roulade is covered with liquid all the time and adding extra water to cover if needed. If you don't have a big enough pan, use a deep roasting tray, one that can hold your belly submerged in liquid, and after bringing to a boil, bake in a preheated oven at 260°F for 5 hours. If you went with the cubes, cook on the burner as for the roulade. In the

For the pork belly

* 2¾ lb prepared and trimmed pork belly (ask your butcher to take the skin off and prep it for you so that it's ready to roll; if you ask nicely, I bet he'll also throw in some butcher's twine so that you can roll it like a pro)
* 2 tbsp turbinado sugar
* 4 tbsp Ras el Hanout Spice Mix (see p.18)
* salt and pepper
* 8 dried apricots
* 8 dried pitted prunes
* 8 dried figs
* 2½ cups water
* ¼ cup canola oil
* 1 carrot, roughly chopped
* 1 onion, roughly chopped
* 1 leek, roughly chopped and well washed
* 1 celery rib, roughly chopped
* 1 unwaxed orange, cut in half
* 1 tsp crushed red pepper flakes
* ¼ cup cold butter, cut into cubes

For the glazed vegetables

* 2 tbsp butter
* 2 tbsp turbinado sugar
* 3 carrots, peeled and cut into rounds ¾ inch thick on the diagonal
* 1 large celery root, peeled and cut into 1-inch cubes (if you have any trimmings, just add them to the pork cooking vegetables)
* 1½ cups pork cooking liquid (see method)

For the Israeli couscous

* ¼ cup canola oil
* 1 large onion, chopped
* 2 garlic cloves, chopped
* 1lb Israeli couscous (if you can get Osem ptitim, it's the best)
* 1 tsp sweet paprika
* salt and pepper
* 1 cup pork cooking liquid (see method; can be replaced with vegetable stock — see p.123 for homemade — if you want to make this as a vegetarian side dish)
* 2½ cups vegetable stock (see p.123 for homemade — can be replaced with water)

restaurant, we cook it overnight in the Josper charcoal oven at 225–250°F for 6–7 hours, and if you have the time and patience, that's my favorite way to go, although both methods work brilliantly.

5. Once cooked, gently remove the roulade from its cooking pan and place on a tray. Leave to cool and then chill in the fridge overnight. Strain the cooking liquid (discard the vegetables, as they have no flavor left), leave to cool and then chill. The liquid contains a large amount of fat, but once chilled the fat will rise to the top and can then be easily skimmed off, ensuring that the liquid is clear and tasty once it's reduced and allow the vegetables to be glazed without unnecessary fat. Set aside 1¼ cups and 1 cup for the glazed vegetables and the Israeli couscous, respectively, and reduce the rest of the liquid by two-thirds. Reduction is the way we intensify flavors, whereby some of the water content is evaporated to leave an enhanced liquid. That's why it's important to add salt only at the end of the process, if needed. Follow the same procedure above if you've gone with the cubes.

6. For the glazed vegetables, heat a large, shallow pan (one that can hold all the vegetables in a single layer, so use 2 pans if necessary) over a medium heat. Add the butter and sugar, then the vegetables.

7. Toss until all the vegetables are coated and then add the pork cooking liquid. Cook for 10 minutes until all the vegetables are glazed and there is almost no liquid in the pan, then set aside. The vegetables need to be slightly undercooked at this point, as they will continue to cook with the belly.

8. For the Israeli couscous, heat a medium-sized pan over a medium heat, add the oil and the onion and sweat for 5 minutes. Add the garlic and couscous and cook, stirring, for another 5 minutes to make sure the oil coats every couscous grain.

9. Add the paprika and season to taste with salt and pepper, then stir in the pork cooking liquid and vegetable stock (or just stock) and bring to a boil. Reduce the heat to a minimum, cover and cook for 7 minutes, stirring from time to time.

10. Take off the heat and leave to rest for 7 more minutes, still covered, then check for seasoning before you serve.

11. To finish the pork, when the couscous is underway, take the roulade (or cubes) out of the fridge, gently cut and remove the twine and then slice into 4. Now it all comes together — we're almost there. Heat a large, heavy-bottomed shallow pan over a high heat, add the rest of the oil and sear the belly for 30 seconds on each side. Reduce the heat and add the remaining reduced cooking liquid, reserved poached dried fruits and the glazed vegetables, making sure you baste the belly continuously. Once the liquid has reduced (after 10 minutes or so), add the crushed red pepper flakes and the butter and shake the pan a bit to incorporate the butter. Check for salt and you're there.

12. To serve, divide the hot Israeli couscous among 4 serving plates and serve the pork and glazed fruits and vegetables on top.

TOMER

I could say I'm more comfortable expressing myself through flavors than words… but who am I kidding? I love to talk. So here are a few things I can tell you about myself and my crazy Palomar journey — grab a beer, kick back and I'll be as succinct as I can!

I was born in Jerusalem and had a great childhood, filled with wonderful food. As well as having fun with my big brothers, I loved going to the Machane Yehuda market with my Kurdish papa, Yoav, and cooking with my Moroccan mama, Sima. At the age of 12, I discovered the guitar and was dead-set on becoming a rock star. I used to cook for my metal band whenever we went camping overnight.

Tomer and Yael

In 2005 I finished my time in the army and was planning to study music the following year in LA. Chef Uri Navon (my brother from another mother) suggested I spend the year in cooking school, since cooking was my other passion. Two weeks into the course, I knew what I wanted to do for the rest of my life — I was falling more deeply in love with cooking with every passing day.

Machneyuda restaurant was opened in Jerusalem in 2009 by Assaf Granit, Yossi "Papi" Elad and Uri Navon, and I became their sous chef. The three years that followed were insanely hectic, and during that time I married my beautiful wife, Yael — it was a huge wedding and the whole Machneyuda team were there. I became the Head Chef of Yuddale, the new restaurant they opened across the street from Machneyuda, and here I got to work side by side with Yael, who became one of the pastry chefs for the Machneyuda group.

We always dreamed of traveling, and when Zoe and Layo came into our lives we knew this was our moment, so we journeyed to London to open The Palomar. Now came the real challenges — new life, language, people, ingredients — it was difficult, but also exciting and truly amazing. Being so far from home gave me the perfect perspective to explore and express my culinary identity, influences and heritage.

And that's me: a dreamer, a big foodaholic, a cook, and someone who likes to talk way too much.

For the lamb shoulder

* 1 lamb shoulder on the bone, about 4½ lb
* 2 tbsp Harissa (see p.27)
* 2 tbsp Cured Lemon Paste (see p.25)
* 1 tbsp toasted and ground cumin seeds
* salt and pepper
* 1 tsp sugar
* 5 garlic cloves, peeled
* 1 onion, cut into quarters
* 1 carrot, roughly chopped
* 2 celery ribs, roughly chopped

To serve

* 6 Kubaneh Breads (see p.230), or any kind of bread or parcel (see recipe introduction), as long as it's carbs!
* 6 tbsp Red Onions and Sumac (see p.33)
* 6 tbsp Tzatziki (see p.38)
* 6 tbsp Schug (see p.34)

Pulled lamb shoulder kubaneh burger

Serves 6 hungry people

This burger was crafted for a pop-up night in London. We wanted to create a nontraditional burger with a nontraditional bun, and what better bun than a soft, rich Kubaneh? The shoulder is a great cut to work with; braising it on the bone gives tons of extra flavor, and it will make you look like a professional chef with no extra effort, plus it's pretty cheap to buy. This recipe works brilliantly as a base for pastas, a filling for ravioli (or kreplach — see p.188–191), as a meat stew or served on plain rice with some of the cooking liquor. Basically, anything goes. Just make sure you plan a day ahead if you want to leave it to rest overnight in the fridge before braising.

As for the bun, you can put the meat in a Pita (see p.229) or flatbread, or between two slices of Challah (see p.238) or even in a regular burger bun. No rules. Also feel free to play with the fillings. This version is my personal favorite, but it's so easy to mix and match with whatever you have available in your fridge.

---

1. Place the shoulder on a deep baking sheet (you will need to cover it later with water, so make sure it's deep enough). Rub lovingly with the Harissa, Cured Lemon Paste, cumin, some salt and pepper and sugar. Pierce the shoulder with a knife in 5 strategic places to make small pockets and insert the garlic cloves (I like to do this with almost any slow-cooked cut). Leave the lamb in the fridge for 4–6 hours, or at room temperature for 2–3 hours if you can't wait. But ideally, you'd give it overnight in the fridge.

2. Preheat your oven to its highest setting, 425°–480°F and roast the shoulder for 15 minutes. Turn it over, add the vegetables and roast for another 15 minutes. Now add water to cover, cover with parchment paper and then foil and return to the oven. (We want to bring the water to a boil first, so if you have a tray that has a flameproof base you can place it on the burner to boil to save you some time.) Check the shoulder after 20–30 minutes, and if the water is boiling, reduce the oven temperature to 250°F and braise for 6–7 hours. If not yet boiled, give it another 10–30 minutes until it does. (Some ovens are more powerful than others, some are less even and so on, but the important thing is to make sure the water boils before you reduce the heat.) If 7 hours is too long, you can instead reduce the temperature to 300–325°F for 3–4 hours.

3. When your shoulder is nice and tender, take it out of the oven and let it cool slightly on a tray. It's best to pull the meat while the shoulder is still hot — it makes the process very easy. Pass the braising liquids through a sieve and set aside.

4. OK so now you have two options:

Option 1 Let's call this the quicker version, translated to "I want my Kubaneh now." Simply heat the pulled lamb shoulder in a pan and let it crisp up a bit, then add 2–3 ladles of the braising liquid. Leave the liquid to be absorbed into the meat for 5–7 minutes, then check for salt and pepper and you're good to go.

Option 2 This is the richer, stronger flavor version and is great to use for pasta (see Variation below) or a stew. Leave the braising liquid to cool, then put it in the fridge until the fat solidifies and then you can easily skim it off. A faster method that I use sometimes is an ice bain-marie: put the liquid in a metal or stainless steel container and submerge in a second container filled with ice. This works well if you have access to loads of ice. Place the skimmed liquid in a pan and reduce by two-thirds. Heat up the pulled lamb shoulder in a pan so it gets crispy, then proceed as in Option 1.

5. Back to our nonconventional burger. Heat your grill to its highest setting. Cut the Kubaneh Breads in half horizontally, place in the oven with the cut sides facing upward and toast for 1–2 minutes. Or if it's a sunny day toast it on the barbecue.

6. To serve, place the onions on the bottom halves of the buns, then add the pulled lamb followed by the Tzatziki. Smear the top halves of Kubaneh with the Schug, pop on the lids and serve.

Variation

For a pasta sauce, follow Option 2 to skim and reduce the braising liquid, then add a pat of butter, some chopped parsley and pine nuts, plus the pulled lamb, of course.

For the cauliflower cream

* 2 tbsp butter
* 1 leek, white part only, sliced and well washed
* 2 sprigs of thyme, chopped
* 1 cauliflower, cut into florets
* salt, to taste
* ¼ cup white wine
* 1¼ cups vegetable stock (see p.123 for homemade) or water
* ⅓ cup heavy cream
* white pepper, to taste (optional)

For the basic freekeh

* 1¾ tbsp butter
* 1 tbsp olive oil, plus an extra drizzle
* 1 small onion, finely diced
* 1 small leek, white part only, well washed and finely diced
* 1½ cups freekeh
* salt, to taste
* 2¼ cups vegetable stock (see p.123 for homemade) or water
* pepper, to taste

→ **Ingredients and recipe continued on next page**

Lamb chops with festive freekeh & cauliflower cream

Serves 4

Lamb and freekeh are an excellent combination. Both ingredients are commonly used in Galilean cooking. The inspiration for the festive freekeh comes from a special rice dish traditionally served at weddings, which is basically white rice with lots of nuts.

The method of prepping the freekeh is a bit unorthodox: a mix between a rice pilaf and a risotto, with the end result being a bit creamy from the starch that the grain releases, which works brilliantly with all the nuts and herbs. You can serve it as a side dish, or even add some butter and Parmesan at the end to make a freekeh risotto.

Start the cauliflower cream and the freekeh at the same time — it will make your life easier.

1. To make the cauliflower cream, heat a pan over a medium heat, add the butter, leek and thyme and sweat for 10 minutes. Then add the cauliflower and sweat for another 7 minutes, stirring occasionally. Season with a little salt.

2. Add the white wine, crank up the heat and cook for another 3–4 minutes, then stir in the stock or water and bring to a boil. Reduce the heat and simmer until the cauliflower is soft — this should take 15–20 minutes.

3. Add the cream and simmer for 5 minutes. Strain off the liquid and transfer the solids to a blender or food processor, then blitz while adding the liquid as you go, stopping when you have achieved a smooth, creamy texture. Don't be afraid of over-blitzing — I like to blitz for 7 minutes on full power to make sure it is super smooth.

4. Strain the cream through a fine sieve, season to taste with salt, and white pepper if you like, and set aside in a saucepan.

5. To make the freekeh, heat up a large saucepan over a medium heat, add the butter, oil, onion and leek and sweat for 10 minutes. Add the freekeh and cook, stirring, for 4–5 minutes — we want to get it coated with the butter and oil. Season with a little salt.

6. Add the stock or water and bring to a boil, then reduce the heat and simmer for 30–40 minutes, stirring every 5 minutes. If at any point you feel that it's getting a bit dry, add a little more stock or water.

7. At this point, your grain should be soft with a touch of crunch at the center — a bit like risotto rice, or al dente as the Italians say. If it's still a bit hard, add some more liquid and continue to cook over a low heat, stirring, until you get there (the cooking time varies with the different kinds and source of the grain).

8. Add all the "festive" nuts and herbs, season to taste with salt and pepper and add a drizzle of olive oil. Set aside until you're ready to serve.

For the "festive" part

* handful of toasted and chopped pistachio nuts (see p.21)
* handful of toasted and chopped blanched almonds (see p.21)
* handful of toasted and chopped pine nuts (see p.21)
* handful of chopped parsley
* handful of chopped mint

For the lamb chops

* 12 lamb chops
* salt and pepper
* handful of chopped thyme
* 4 tbsp olive oil
* 1 tbsp canola oil

To serve

* ¼ cup Watercress Pesto (see p.31)
* handful of micro parsley (optional)

9. For the lamb chops: there are different cooking methods to choose from here. In the restaurant, we grill them in a charcoal grill for a great smokiness and charcoal flavor. You could cook them on an outdoor barbecue, grill them in the oven or fry them in a pan on the burner — all will work great, but just make sure that you follow one principle: hot and fast.

10. Season your chops on a tray with all the ingredients, rubbing them in well.

11. To pan-fry, heat 2–3 large skillets until they are blazing hot and sear the chops for 2–3 minutes on each side, adding the excess oil left in the tray to the pans — the cooking time will vary according to the size of the chops and the firepower you have, so don't be shy to add an extra minute if you feel they need it. The chops should be pink but not bleeding; a touch above medium. Remove from the pans to a tray and leave to rest while you serve up the other elements. To grill or barbecue, preheat your grill, or a barbecue, to a high heat and cook in the same way as above — hot and quick! Remove from the grill or barbecue and leave to rest as above.

12. To serve, heat up the cauliflower cream and divide between the serving plates. Top each plate with the freekeh and place 3 chops on each plate. Garnish each chop with a teaspoon of Watercress Pesto, and finish with the micro parsley, if you like.

Variations

The cauliflower cream is great for serving with all kinds of meat, fish and seafood, and if you loosen it a little with more liquid, you have a tasty cauliflower soup.

Lambs' tongues with tirshi, spinach & bok choy

Serves 4

First of all, relax: lambs' tongues are tasty, healthy and super-easy and quick to cook. Now that we've got that out of the way, I can also tell you that they are really tender when prepared properly and have a delicate flavor to rival any other cut of lamb. This quasi salad, which brings together lots of temperatures, textures and flavors, was created as a special in the restaurant, and it was so popular that we had to bring it back several times.

---

1. Start with the tongues. Place them in a pan large enough to fit them all with some room to spare, cover with water and add the bay leaves (if using) and vinegar. Bring to a boil, then reduce the heat and simmer for 1½ hours. Pierce with a knife to make sure they're tender enough — the knife should slide in easily. Some tongues are bigger (depending on the age of the lamb), so you may need to cook them for up to an extra 30 minutes.

2. Once the tongues are cooked, drain and then peel off the rough membrane under running water — you can just use your fingers, as they should be really easy to peel. Cut the peeled tongues into ⅜-inch slices.

3. For the salad, mix the spinach, bok choy leaves, red onion and radishes in a bowl and set aside.

4. Fry the tongues in the olive oil in a large, wide, shallow pan over a medium-high heat for 2 minutes and season with some salt. Add the white parts of the bok choy (and if you have any spinach stalks, those as well) and cook for about another 2–3 minutes until the tongues have a nice golden brown color, then add the Harissa, Garlic Confit (if using), spices and butter. Stir a little to give you a nice red shiny sauce and add a squeeze of lemon juice just at the end.

5. Let the mixture cool for about 2–3 minutes — you still want it warm but not enough to kill the leaves — then add to the salad in the mixing bowl. Dress with the lemon juice and olive oil, season with salt and mix quickly, then check one last time for salt.

6. Let's plate: divide the yogurt between the serving plates and make a nice well in the middle, add the Tirshi in the middle and mash it a bit. Then divide the salad among the plates, on top of the Tirshi, and garnish with the toasted slivered almonds.

For the lambs' tongues

* 1¾ lb lambs' tongues
* 2 bay leaves (optional)
* 2 tbsp white wine vinegar
* 1 tbsp olive oil
* salt, to taste
* 2 tbsp Harissa (see p.27)
* 6 Garlic Confit Cloves (see p.46), optional
* 1 tsp toasted and ground coriander seeds
* ½ tsp toasted and ground cumin seeds
* 1 tbsp butter
* squeeze of lemon juice

For the salad

* About 1lb spinach, washed and dried (baby spinach is ideal; if using wild or Turkish spinach, remove the stalks, chop them and throw them in with the bok choy, then just roughly chop the leaves)
* 2 heads of bok choy, green parts only, roughly chopped, white parts sliced and reserved for the tongues
* 1 small red onion, cut in half and thinly sliced
* 4 French radishes, thinly sliced
* 2 tbsp freshly squeezed lemon juice
* 1 tbsp olive oil
* salt, to taste

To serve

* 6 large tbsp Greek yogurt
* 6 large tbsp Tirshi (see p.63)
* generous handful of toasted
  slivered almonds (see p.21)

Bumblebee
See cocktail insert for recipe

Jerusalem mix with okra

Serves 4

Apparently, this dish was born on Agripas Street in Machane Yehuda market in 1969. Traditionally it is a mix of chicken hearts, livers, thighs and spleen (although you can use different cuts) seared on the plancha (griddle) with lots of sliced onions and spices, all of which then goes into a pita. Legend has it that the first one was made by mistake (often the way with ingenious creations): it's a rainy night on Agripas Street and the charcoal grill at Haim's little meat stand is already cold when a customer arrives and asks for something to eat. So he improvises with a shallow can on an old stove used to heat Turkish coffee, takes apart a couple of skewers, tosses the meat medley with some onions and spices in the can and the first Jerusalem Mix is born.

Here, many years later, I've tried to pay my respects to the famous dish. This take is with okra and burned tomatoes, and I've also added some sweetbreads, but feel free to play with the mix meat-wise. As I said before, it doesn't have to be offal — you can go for chopped boneless chicken thighs or breasts or even chopped flank or skirt steak — it's the seasoning and loads of onion that are the most important ingredients.

———

A few words about sweetbreads before we start. These come from two different parts of the animal, the neck area (thymus gland) and the stomach area (pancreas). The former, considered to be the more luxurious, are fatty and soft, usually used for grilling with a touch of lemon juice and involve no initial preparation other than a good cleaning from your butcher. The latter are more common and the ones used here, which require a bit of simple pre-prepping.

1. Soak the sweetbreads in iced water for 15 minutes, then remove and gently simmer them in the vinegar in a saucepan for 6–7 minutes. Return to the iced water for 10 minutes, then drain, peel off the membranes and slice into ½-inch pieces.

2. Place the okra in a large cold pan (a sauteuse is perfect if you have one) and set over a medium heat on the burner. We want to sear all the tiny hairs off the okra and to crisp it up, so toss it around in the pan.

3. When the pan is hot, take the okra out, add half the oils and all the onions and season with some salt and pepper and one-quarter of the Jerusalem Spice Mix. Crank the heat up and fry the onions to a nice color.

4. Return the okra to the pan and toss for another 2–3 minutes, then take it out again, for two reasons: one, we don't want it to burn; two, we need to make room for the offal to be seared properly. So now season the offal with salt and pepper and the rest of the Jerusalem Spice Mix, and make sure your pan is hot hot hot! Add the remaining oils to the pan, then the offal and sear on both sides for a minute.

---

* ½ lb veal or lamb sweetbreads
* 2 tbsp white wine or cider vinegar
* ½ lb okra
* 3 tbsp canola oil
* 3 tbsp olive oil
* 2 large white onions, sliced
* salt and pepper
* 1 tbsp Jerusalem Spice Mix (see p.18)
* About ⅔ lb chicken livers, cleaned and trimmed
* About ⅔ lb chicken hearts, cleaned and trimmed (cut in half, wash and dry well)
* 8 Garlic Confit Cloves (see p.46)
* 12 cherry tomatoes, charred over an open flame on the burner or barbecue for 3–4 minutes until blackened all over
* handful of chopped parsley
* handful of chopped cilantro
* pinch of crushed red pepper flakes
* squeeze of lemon juice

To serve

* 4 tbsp Greek yogurt
* 4 tsp Schug (see p.34)
* 4 tbsp White Tahini Sauce
  (see p.28)
* handful of cilantro leaves

5. Add the Garlic Confit, tomatoes, onions and okra, and toss together — the aroma should make you really hungry. Then add the herbs, crushed red pepper flakes and squeeze of lemon juice, and check for seasoning.

6. To serve, drizzle the yogurt and Schug around the outside of 4 serving plates, spoon some White Tahini Sauce into the middle, then the meat mix on top and finally garnish with the cilantro leaves.

Wedding veal brain with peppers & chickpeas

Serves 4

I loved weddings growing up in the '80s and '90s. You would see all your extended family, eat a lot and dance yourself silly. Another thing you could rely on was the food — you always had the same three starters and the same three mains to choose from, no matter which town the wedding took place. The starter that especially intrigued me as a child was pan-fried veal brain in a traditional Moroccan red pepper and chickpea stew. Brain was not something you ate at my house on a regular basis, so weddings were my only opportunity to enjoy it.

For this recipe, I've played around with different peppers and spice levels to create a depth and complexity of heat to the dish. My grandma used to make it with only paprika and dried chiles and it was super hot, whereas here I've used red peppers to balance the heat. But you can add or subtract the chile heat as you like.

———————

1. To pre-prepare the brain, make sure it is cold from the fridge (brain freeze!), which will help it to stay firm during the whole process. Bring the 12 cups of water to a boil in a large pan, add the bay leaves and vinegar and then the brain and simmer gently for 5–7 minutes. The brain should be firm but yielding — if it's still too wobbly, poach it for another 2–3 minutes. Meanwhile, fill a large bowl with plenty of iced water (ensure that it's really icy, which will make the task of peeling away the membranes very easy). Once the brain is ready, transfer it to the iced water and shake quickly to halt cooking.

2. When the brain is completely cold and firm, remove it from the iced water and pat dry gently with paper towels, then peel off the membranes delicately — you don't need to peel them all away, just the thicker ones. Cut the brain into 4 equal bite-sized pieces and keep dry and covered in the fridge while you cook the pepper stew.

3. For the vegetable stew, heat a large pan over a medium to high heat, add the oil and red peppers with a pinch of salt and let them sweat for 12–15 minutes — they need to tenderize but stay firm.

4. Add the garlic and chiles, then reduce the heat to medium, add ½ teaspoon of each spice and cook, stirring often, for 5–7 minutes. Add the tomatoes and simmer for 20 minutes.

5. Stir in the chickpeas, half the cilantro, the remaining spices and the sugar, and simmer for another 10 minutes. If the stew starts to dry out at any stage, add a little water or vegetable stock. Now turn off the heat and leave the stew to rest so that the flavors settle.

* About 1lb veal brain (ask your butcher for fresh, clean brain; if you can get hold of lambs' brains, you've really hit the jackpot, as they are very tender with a delicate flavor)
* 12 cups water
* 2 bay leaves
* 2 tbsp white wine vinegar
* 4 tbsp all-purpose flour
* 2 eggs, lightly beaten
* salt and pepper
* pinch of crushed red pepper flakes (optional, but I like it spicy)
* 1⅓ cups golden bread crumbs or panko (to give the crust a nice airy texture)
* 6⅓ cups canola oil, for deep-frying

For the stew

* 4 tbsp olive oil
* 3 red peppers, cored, seeded and cut into ⅝–¾-inch fingers, or ¾-inch cubes if you prefer
* salt
* 6 garlic cloves, sliced
* 2 dried red chiles, soaked in water for 20 minutes (optional or can be replaced with 1 tbsp Harissa, p.27)
* 1–2 green or red chiles, sliced (depending on how spicy you like it; I like it spicy, so I go for 2 red)
* 1½ tbsp sweet paprika
* 1 tsp toasted and ground cumin seeds
* 1 tsp toasted and ground coriander seeds
* 1 tsp hot paprika (optional)
* 4 ripe tomatoes, skinned and cut into ¾-inch cubes (can be replaced with a 14.5oz can good-quality chopped tomatoes)
* ½ cup dried chickpeas, soaked overnight in 4¼ cups cold water, then drained, cooked in 12 cups water for 2–3 hours until tender yet firm and drained again
* 2 handfuls of chopped cilantro
* 1 tsp sugar
* 3 tbsp freshly squeezed lemon juice

6. Next, we'll fry the brain, beginning with breading it. Take the brain out of the fridge. Place the flour and beaten eggs in separate shallow bowls and season both with salt, pepper and the optional crushed red pepper flakes. Place the bread crumbs in a third bowl. Coat each piece of brain first in flour, then the eggs and finally in the bread crumbs. Heat the oil for deep-frying in a deep saucepan to 340–350°F (see p.55 if you don't have a thermometer). Deep-fry the brain pieces, one at a time, for 1–3 minutes until nice and golden brown. Remove from the oil and pat dry on paper towels, then season with some salt.

7. While you're deep-frying the brain, turn the heat back on under the stew. Add the lemon juice and the rest of the cilantro, and check for salt.

8. To serve, divide the stew between 4 serving plates and place a piece of brain in the center of each plate. Wait for the reactions from your guests, then pull the rabbit out of the hat and tell them what they're having.

Chicken livers in date syrup & bourbon with mash

Serves 4

This quick and easy recipe makes an excellent lunch dish. The date syrup and bourbon are really great friends and make a perfect match for creamy mash. Make sure you get nice, fat fresh livers so that you can happily cook them to medium; for me, well-done livers are a big turn-off. This recipe is another creative way to elevate an affordable ingredient to its full potential.

———

Start cooking the onions and the mash at the same time and you'll be eating within an hour.

1. To make the onions in bourbon, preheat the oven to 375°F. Arrange the onion "steaks" in a single layer in a baking sheet large enough to hold them with their cooking liquid.

2. Season with some salt and pepper and thyme, add the stock or water and bourbon, then drizzle the date syrup all over the onions. Place a cube of butter on each onion and cover with foil.

3. Bake for 20 minutes, then lift off the foil and bake for another 10 minutes. Remove from the oven and set aside, still in the liquid — they should be caramelized.

4. To make the creamy mash, cook the potatoes (skins on), in a large pan of salted boiling water for about 30 minutes until they're soft. Drain and, while still fairly hot, peel them.

5. Pass through a moulin à légumes if you have one. This is a nice French word for a food mill, and I really recommend getting one — you can easily find cute home-kitchen-sized ones now and they're great fun to use. But if you don't have one, you can use a fine sieve — it takes a bit more time but you will achieve the same aim, which is to have our mash creamy and smooth.

6. Meanwhile, combine the milk and cream and heat in a pan on the burner or in the microwave in a microwave-proof bowl.

7. Place the mash in a saucepan and fold in the butter, cube by cube, with a spatula over a low heat. Once the texture is smooth, add the hot milk and cream mixture little by little using a whisk, which will give you a creamy, almost ice cream–like texture. Season to taste with salt and set aside.

8. For the livers, heat up 2 large skillets over a high heat, and season the livers with salt and pepper. Once the pans are really hot, add half the butter divided between the 2 pans. Add the livers, making sure they are in a single layer, and sear for 1 minute on each side. Be careful, as livers have a tendency to pop some butter while you sear them — but don't be afraid, just be aware.

For the onions in bourbon

* 3 large red onions, cut into "steaks" or rounds ¾ inch thick
* salt and pepper, to taste
* 2 tbsp thyme leaves
* ¼ cup vegetable stock (see p.123 for homemade) or chicken stock or water
* 5 tbsp bourbon
* ¼ cup date syrup
* 2 tbsp butter, cut into cubes

For the creamy mash

* 2 large potatoes, skin on, about 1lb–1⅓lb in total, washed
* salt
* ¼ cup milk
* ¼ cup heavy cream
* ½ cup butter, cut into cubes

For the livers

* 1½ lb trimmed chicken livers
  (ask your butcher to trim them
  if you're not sure how)
* salt and pepper, to taste
* ⅓ cup butter, cut into cubes
* ¼ cup bourbon (my preferred
  tipple is Jack Daniel's)
* ¼ cup vegetable stock (see
  p.123 for homemade) or
  chicken stock or water
* ¼ cup date syrup
* 8 Garlic Confit Cloves
  (see p.46)
* handful of Curly Scallions (see
  p.85), to garnish

9. Divide the bourbon between the 2 pans and shake a little to flambé, then add the stock or water and deglaze the base of the pan with a wooden spoon.

10. Add the onions with their liquid, the date syrup and the Garlic Confit and reduce for 2–3 minutes, then add the rest of the butter and season to taste with salt and pepper.

11. To serve, all that's left to do is to divide up the mash between the serving plates, top with the livers and garnish with the Curly Scallions.

Bad Jew's kreplach

With onion cream, crispy shallots & chrain oil

Serves 6

Kreplach is a traditional dumpling from the Ashkenazi Polish kitchen, which is usually filled with mashed potatoes or ground meat. There are two traditional ways to serve it — either poached and then pan-fried to crisp up with lots of caramelized onions, or poached in a chicken broth in a similar way to that other Ashkenazi favorite, matzoh balls or kneidlach. So why "Bad Jew's Kreplach?" The answer is in the filling: ground pork. The rest of the recipe is a play on the classic fried version of the dish.

— — —

1. For the kreplach, start by making the kreplach dough, then while that's resting, prepare the filling. Heat a large pan over a high heat, add the oil and then the ground pork and cook, breaking it up and stirring constantly with a wooden spoon so that the texture is even, for about 5–10 minutes until browned.

2. Season generously with pepper, add the spices, then season to taste with salt. Set aside to cool, then cover and chill in the fridge until you're ready to fill the kreplach.

3. Again, follow the kreplach recipe on p.242 to fill your kreplach dough with love (and the ground pork filling!), creating half-moon shapes.

4. For the onion cream, heat a large saucepan over a medium heat, add the oil, butter and the onions and sauté for 15 minutes to make sure your onions soften up, stirring occasionally.

5. Add the vinegar, white wine and sugar and cook for 10 minutes. Stir in the vegetable stock or water and cook until the liquid has reduced by half, then add the cream and leave to boil for 2–3 minutes. Take off the heat.

6. Strain off half the liquid and set aside, then transfer the rest of the contents of the pan to a food processor or blender and blitz, adding a little of the reserved liquid, until you have a smooth texture. Pass through a sieve and season to taste with salt, and the white pepper if you like. Set aside.

7. For the crispy shallots, combine the flour and cornstarch in a bowl, add the shallots and toss to coat well. Then transfer the shallots to a sieve and shake to get rid of any excess flour.

8. Heat the oil for deep-frying in a deep saucepan to 325–340°F. Deep-fry the shallots, in small batches, for 2–3 minutes until golden brown. Remove from the oil and drain on a tray lined with paper towels, then season to taste with salt while still hot.

9. To finish, blanch the kreplach in a large saucepan of salted boiling water for 2 minutes, then drain and set aside.

10. Meanwhile, warm the onion cream in a pan, and heat 2 large nonstick skillets for the kreplach over a medium heat. Split the butter between the pans and add the kreplach, making sure that they're not too cramped. Fry for 2–4 minutes, then flip and

---

For the kreplach

* 1 recipe of kreplach dough (see p.242)
* 3 tbsp canola oil
* ¾ lb ground pork (it should contain 15–20% fat)
* pepper
* ½ nutmeg, freshly grated (if you can't get whole nutmeg, use ¼ tsp ground nutmeg)
* ½ tsp ground cloves
* salt, to taste
* 2 tbsp butter

For the onion cream

* 1 tbsp olive oil
* 2 tbsp butter
* 4 onions, sliced
* 2 tbsp white wine vinegar
* ¼ cup white wine
* pinch of sugar
* ¾ cup vegetable stock (see p.123 for homemade) or water
* ½ cup heavy cream
* salt, to taste
* pinch of ground white pepper (optional)

For the crispy shallots

* 1 tbsp all-purpose flour
* 1 tbsp cornstarch
* 2 banana shallots, thinly sliced (use a mandoline to make your life easier)
* 3½ cups canola oil, for deep-frying
* salt, to taste

For the garnish

* 2 tbsp Chrain (see p.33) or finely grated horseradish, mixed thoroughly with 2 tbsp canola oil
* handful of Parmesan cheese shavings (Parmigiano Reggiano or Grana Padano)

crisp up the other side for another 2–4 minutes. Remove from the pans and place gently on a tray lined with paper towels.

11. To serve, put some onion cream on each plate, then the kreplach. Garnish with the Chrain or horseradish oil, then the Parmesan shavings and crispy shallots.

Labneh kreplach tortellini

In a Middle Eastern borscht
Serves 6

Sometimes Middle Eastern flavors and Ashkenazi flavors are a match made in heaven. Ashkenazi borscht is often quite a meaty soup, but I wanted to give it some magic for all you vegetable lovers. Here it gets a rose petal and cumin twist, and instead of the fermented beet juice customarily used, I've added some pomegranate molasses, and the usual sour cream to serve is replaced with my zesty labneh kreplach with Za'atar Spice Mix.

For the kreplach

* 1¼ cups Labneh (see p.41)
* 1 tbsp Za'atar Spice Mix (see p.20)
* 1 tsp grated lemon zest
* salt, to taste
* 1 recipe of kreplach dough (see p.242)

For the borscht

* 4 large beets, skin on, washed and patted dry, then rubbed with 2 tbsp olive oil and baked in the oven (see p.194)
* 2 tbsp olive oil
* 1 onion, sliced
* 1 tbsp dried rose petals
* 1½ tbsp untoasted cumin seeds
* 1 tbsp untoasted coriander seeds
* 7 cups vegetable stock (see p.123 for homemade) or water
* salt and pepper, to taste
* 2 tbsp pomegranate molasses
* parsley leaves, to garnish

1. To make the kreplach filling, mix all the kreplach ingredients except the dough in a bowl, then transfer to a piping bag — this will make it easier to fill the kreplach evenly. Follow the kreplach recipe on p. 242 to fill your dough, shaping the dumplings tortellini style.

2. For the borscht, while your beets are baking, heat a large pan over a medium heat, add the olive oil, onion, rose petals and spices and sauté gently for about 25–30 minutes until caramelized. Add the stock or water and bring to a boil, then reduce the heat and simmer for 15 minutes.

3. Once your beets are cooked, remove them from the oven and leave to cool to room temperature. Then put on some gloves to save staining your hands, peel the foil off — the skin should come off easily with it — and cut into fairly big chunks, about 2 inches in size.

4. Add the beets to the broth and bring to a boil, then simmer for 10 minutes. Season to taste with salt and a generous amount of pepper and stir in the pomegranate molasses. Transfer to a blender or food processor and blitz for 7–10 minutes until smooth. Pass through a sieve and return to the pan for final heating and seasoning.

5. To finish, there are 2 ways you can go here, and both work excellently:

Option 1 Simmer the kreplach in the soup for 5–7 minutes (they will take on a rich purple color), then serve.

Option 2 Blanch the kreplach in a large saucepan of salted boiling water for 3–4 minutes, and while you do that, heat up the soup. Then drain the kreplach and add to the soup when you are ready to serve. This option keeps the flavors a bit more distinct.

6. I like to garnish this dish with parsley leaves, deep-fried for 10 seconds, drained on paper towels, then seasoned with salt, but feel free to try anything from toasted chopped nuts (see p.21 — pine nuts, walnuts and hazelnuts are brilliant for this one); chopped fresh herbs, or even some nice cheese (Pecorino or Parmesan always work for me).

MY DAY AT THE RESTAURANT

by Zoe Paskin

Even when a restaurant is not welcoming the public, it has a daily working rhythm that lasts nearly 24 hours. By the time the kitchen porter has returned the last of the galaxy of kitchen implements to their butcher's hooks, it will be past 2am. The closing manager presses "send" on the nightly report, makes their closing checks and finally locks up — then, within a couple of hours, the cleaners come to prepare the space for the new day. Shortly after that, one of our pastry chefs arrives to bake our kubaneh bread, and the full team clocks in by 8am.

As a child, I always loved the feeling when one of my parents was preparing for friends to come for supper — the feeling of anticipation, as kirs were drunk, Gitanes smoked and one of my nanas was cooking up one of their specialities. I loved licking the bowl or watching the delicate construction of a Swiss roll — coming from a very foodie home, Layo and I both adapted quickly, and baking, marinating, roasting, searing, frying all became second nature to us. That excited feeling comes back to me at The Palomar on a daily basis. It begins early morning when arriving in Soho and

Zoe at The Palomar, 2015

seeing the city come to life. An espresso at the bar, watching the meat, the catch of the day, the fresh fruit, vegetables and herbs arrive — the child in me feels like we're gearing up for a giant family feast. I'll breeze around the restaurant full of *bonhomie* to lift the spirits and "mother" the team, greeting each of them personally. I may find Papi preparing sardines, or exchange a knowing look or share a joke with one of our chefs. The Palomar has a family feel. I've worked with my brother for most of my career — he's my business partner and my best friend — and this family feeling runs through our whole team. Many of us have worked together at different times and places over the years — our people are our lifeblood. We're meticulous about details and each member of our team is the kind of person who strives for perfection, but ultimately it is this warmth and passion that defines us. And this is what we want to give you, in our restaurant, each time you join us.

Beet filled with ground lamb
See p.194–5

Beet filled with ground lamb

Serves 4

A very talented and slightly crazy Argentinian cook, Lucas Zitrinovich, was my first sous chef back when I was young and foolish. When we worked together at Machneyuda, he came up with this tasty dish. It tasted so Levantine that you could have sworn he was born in Beirut and not in sweet Corrientes. As with many of our recipes, I recommend that you cook both elements simultaneously to speed up the whole process.

---

1. For the filling, heat a large pan over a medium heat, add the oil and the onion and season with half the spices and some salt and pepper. Sauté for about 10–15 minutes until caramelized, then add the garlic and celery and cook, stirring, for 3–4 minutes.

2. Add the ground lamb, crank up the heat to high and cook, breaking it up and stirring constantly with a wooden spoon so that the texture is even, for about 5–10 minutes until browned. Season with the rest of the spices, salt and pepper, tasting to see if you're happy with the seasoning, then transfer to a bowl and leave to cool.

3. For the beet, preheat your oven to 350°F. Rub the beets with the olive oil and wrap each of them individually in foil — baking them in their skins and the foil will ensure that the beets cook perfectly and that the flavor is intense and bright. Place on a baking sheet and bake for 1 hour. To check that they're cooked through, pierce with a knife — if it slides in easily, they're done, but if not, give them an extra 10–30 minutes (some beets are gigantic).

4. Once cooked, remove the beets from the oven and leave to cool to room temperature. Put on some gloves to save staining your hands, peel the foil off — the skin should come off easily with it — and slice about ¾–1¼ inches off the top (you can keep these lids for replacing later if you like), plus a tiny bit off the bottom just so that they stand nicely. Using a teaspoon, gently scoop out the insides of the beets and set aside. I like to mix the cooked beet flesh with some lemon juice, olive oil, salt, pepper and a touch of toasted and ground cumin seeds and crushed red pepper flakes, which makes a perfect nibble or a mezze (this works amazingly well with raw beets too). Meanwhile, back to the hollowed-out beets.

5. Increase your oven temperature to 375°F. Mix all the remaining beet ingredients except the seasoning and butter together and rub the mixture with love over the inside and outside of the beets, standing on the baking sheet. Then season to taste with salt and pepper, divide the 1½ tbsp butter into quarters and place one-quarter inside each beet. You will have a lot of liquid in the tray, but that's good because it will form our sauce later on. Bake the beets for 5 minutes, then remove the tray from the oven and fill with the ground lamb mixture — you can replace the tops, but I like to keep mine open. Pop back in the oven for another 5 minutes.

For the filling

* 3 tbsp olive oil
* 1 onion, diced
* 1–2 tsp Baharat Spice Mix (see p.20), optional
* 1 tsp toasted and ground cumin seeds
* 1 tsp toasted and ground coriander seeds
* salt and pepper, to taste
* 2 garlic cloves, finely chopped
* 1 celery rib, diced
* ½ lb ground lamb (I like it with 15–20% fat)

For the beets

* 4 large beets, skin on, washed and patted dry
* 2 tbsp olive oil
* 2 tbsp date syrup
* 2 tbsp pomegranate molasses
* 1 tsp Harissa (see p.27)
* ½ cup vegetable stock (see p.123 for homemade) or water
* salt and pepper, to taste
* 1½ tbsp butter, plus an extra 2 tbsp to serve

For the garnish

* 4 large tbsp Greek yogurt
* handful of micro cilantro or any other herb you like, such as parsley or mint, or a mixture of all of them
* 1 radish, thinly sliced
* 1 tbsp olive oil
* squeeze of lemon juice
* salt, to taste

6. To serve, divide the yogurt between the serving plates, making a nice well in the middle for the beets to sit in. Dress the herbs and sliced radish with the olive oil, lemon juice and salt to taste, and place next to the yogurt.

7. Take the beets out of the oven and place one on each plate. Add the remaining 2 tbsp butter to the beet baking sheet and incorporate with a wooden spoon — if the sauce is too thick, add a touch of water. Drizzle a little sauce over each beet and serve.

THE PASTRY ROOM

In a restaurant the pastry room is usually an isolated kingdom ruled over by the pastry chef, and anyone who tries to invade the space would most likely get the evil eye. But that's not the case at The Palomar. We have a small restaurant and therefore a small pastry area; it doesn't even have a door. And so, like a family, we are forced to share it all — the good, the bad and the in-between — as though we were at home.

Another similarity to home baking is that you don't need elaborate equipment to make the recipes in this book. The most important items in a pastry chef's toolkit are simple measuring utensils — so if you don't already have them, get a digital scale and a measuring cup. With these, plus a decent spatula and a good-quality whisk, you're ready to go. (Don't say no if you're offered a stand mixer, though!)

How should you approach the recipes in this chapter? First, relax and remember that baking is fun. Second, you'll find that every dessert is built from a basic recipe along with my suggestion of how to finish it off like we do at The Palomar. This means that, if you prefer, you can just make the basic recipe for a particular dessert and serve it as it is or with any topping/side you like. Alternatively, you can go the whole nine yards and try the full-on version. The important thing is just to play and have fun with it.

by Yael Vardi

Orange blossom ice cream in kataifi nests

Serves 10

I'm a big ice cream fan. You don't need an ice cream machine at home to make great ice cream. This recipe really feels like cheating, as it literally takes no more than 15 minutes to make (but then a few good hours of staring in anticipation at the freezer door until it's ready). You can replace the orange blossom with other flavor essences, such as rose water, or replace both the oil and orange blossom water with ½ cup of a spread, such as peanut butter, chocolate hazelnut spread and so on.

For the orange blossom ice cream

* 1¾ cups condensed milk
* 1 tbsp orange blossom water
* 5 tbsp vegetable oil
* 2¼ cups whipping cream

For the kataifi nests

* ¼ lb kataifi pastry (shredded filo pastry dough)
* 3 tbsp confectioners' sugar, sifted
* 2½ tbsp butter, melted

To serve

* 2 oranges
* Orange Syrup (see p.208–210)
* handful of toasted slivered almonds

1. To make the orange blossom ice cream, mix the condensed milk, orange blossom water and oil together in a mixing bowl using a whisk.

2. In a separate bowl, whip the cream to soft peaks, then gently fold the cream into the condensed milk mixture.

3. Transfer the mixture to a lidded freezer-proof container and leave in the freezer for at least 6 hours, or overnight. That's it! Easy! The ice cream can be kept in the freezer for up to 2 weeks.

4. To make the kataifi nests, preheat your oven to 400°F. Separate the kataifi strands and toss with the confectioners' sugar in a mixing bowl until evenly coated. Add the melted butter and mix so that the kataifi are evenly coated in the butter.

5. Divide the kataifi between 10 cups of a cupcake tin, lining each cup with a thin layer of the kataifi. Bake for 7–10 minutes until golden brown.

6. Remove from the oven and leave to cool completely before unmoulding the cups.

7. To serve, cut off the top and bottom of each orange with a serrated knife. Sit the fruit on the chopping board and cut away the rind and white pith from the top to the bottom, turning the fruit around until only the flesh is left (we don't want any white pith, as it is bitter). Cut between the membranes to extract the pristine, pith-free segments.

8. To serve put a nice scoop of the ice cream into each of the kataifi nests. Add an orange segment to each, drizzle over a little Orange Syrup and sprinkle with the slivered almonds.

Vanilla & caramelized pine nut ice cream

With hazelnut tuile & apple caramel

Makes 3½ pints

When Tomer and I first moved in together, a long time before I became a pastry chef, I made this dessert to celebrate. I went off to work excited to know if it had worked. But by the time I got back home it was all gone! So I guess he thought it was a success... I love this frozen dessert for its crunchy bits — definitely my favorite for eating straight from the tub.

---

1. For the vanilla and caramelized pine nut ice cream, first make a caramel by heating a heavy-bottomed nonstick pan over a low heat and add the granulated sugar in one even layer. It's important not to stir or move the pan. Once all the sugar has melted and you have a light caramel, take the pan off the heat, stir in the pine nuts and then transfer to a tray lined with parchment paper. Leave to cool completely, then chop roughly and set aside for later.

2. Whisk the egg whites in a large mixing bowl to soft peaks, then transfer to another large, clean mixing bowl.

3. Whisk the egg yolks, superfine sugar and vanilla together in the bowl that you used for the egg whites (no need to wash) until tripled in size and very pale in color with a creamy texture. Fold in the egg whites.

4. Whip the cream to soft peaks in the bowl that you used for the egg whites (again, no need to wash) and fold into the egg mixture. Then gently fold in the alcohol and caramelized pine nuts. Transfer the mixture to a lidded freezer-proof container and leave in the freezer for at least 6 hours, or overnight. The ice cream can be kept in the freezer for up to 2 weeks.

5. For the apple caramel, heat the sugar until you have a light caramel, as you did for the ice cream above. Add the butter and mix to combine using a whisk — but be careful, as it may spit due to the temperature difference.

6. Add the apple juice, a tablespoonful at a time, again being very careful. Only add more juice once the first addition is combined — if you add too much in one go, it will cool the caramel and leave you with apple juice and lumps of hard caramel!

7. After all the juice has been combined, move the mixture to a container and leave to cool. It's better to store this at room temperature (it will set in the fridge). It will keep for up to 1 week.

8. For the hazelnut tuile, preheat your oven to 375°F and line a baking sheet with parchment paper.

For the vanilla & caramelized pine nut ice cream

* 2½ tbsp granulated sugar
* ⅓ cup toasted pine nuts (see p.21)
* 4 eggs, separated
* ¼ cup superfine sugar
* 1 tsp vanilla extract
* 2¼ cups whipping cream
* 2 tbsp liqueur or rum (don't skip this — the alcohol helps it not to freeze solid)

For the apple caramel

* ½ cup granulated sugar
* small pat of butter
* 4 tbsp unsweetened apple juice

For the hazelnut tuile

* 2 egg whites
* ½ tsp salt
* ¼ cup all-purpose flour
* ¼ cup ground almonds
* ¼ cup butter, melted
* handful of hazelnuts, toasted and chopped (see p.21)
* 1 tbsp turbinado sugar

9. Mix the egg whites and salt together in a mixing bowl until combined — the easiest way is to use a whisk, but we don't want to beat the mixture, just combine it. Mix in the flour and ground almonds, followed by the melted butter.

10. Spread the mixture thinly over the lined baking sheet using a palette knife, then scatter with the chopped hazelnuts and sugar. Bake for 7 minutes or until golden brown. Remove from the oven and leave to cool completely, then break up into pieces and transfer to an airtight container. It will keep for up to 1 month.

11. To serve, simply scoop the ice cream into serving bowls, drizzle with the caramel and sprinkle with tuile pieces.

Variation

For a savory hazelnut tuile — a perfect accompaniment to the Seared Scallops with Cured Lemon Beurre Blanc (see p.132), simply omit the sugar.

Tahini ice cream

With cardamom crème Anglaise, phyllo tuile & fig brûlée

Serves 8

The person who (unknowingly) introduced me to this excellent ice cream was none other than chef Assaf Granit. I was 16 when I ate in the first restaurant where he was a chef, the renowned Adom in Jerusalem. This dessert was on the menu and I remember thinking to myself, "Really? Ice cream from tahini? That's so weird, I have to try it." At that time I had no idea tahini could be eaten with anything else but falafel. So I tried it and it was amazing! Ten years passed and I found myself working as a pastry chef at Machneyuda making the same recipe (good ones last forever). So when we opened The Palomar, I knew I had to create a dessert with it.

For the tahini ice cream

* 1¼ cups whipping cream
* 1¼ cups heavy cream
* ½ cup egg yolks (6–7 eggs)
* ½ cup date syrup
* ½ cup honey
* 1⅔ cups tahini paste

For the cardamom Anglaise

* ¾ cup milk
* ¼ cup heavy cream
* ¼ cup granulated sugar
* 2 cardamom pods, bruised
* 3¼ tbsp egg yolks (3–4)

For the phyllo tuile

* 2 standard-sized sheets of phyllo pastry (19 x 10 inches)
* 2 tbsp butter, melted
* 1 tsp granulated sugar
* 1 tsp ground cinnamon
* ½ tsp turbinado sugar

For the fig brûlée

* 6 figs
* 3 tbsp granulated sugar

1. To make the tahini ice cream, place both the creams in a saucepan and bring to a simmer, then remove from the heat. Place the egg yolks in a bowl and slowly add one-third of the simmering cream while constantly whisking, being careful not to cook the yolks. Now that your cream and yolks are almost at the same temperature, it will be easy to combine them without cooking the yolks, so gradually add the egg yolks back to the saucepan, again while constantly whisking. Next, whisk in the date syrup and honey, then the tahini paste.

2. Transfer the mixture to a lidded freezer-proof container and leave in the freezer overnight. The ice cream can be kept in the freezer for up to 3 months.

3. To make the cardamom Anglaise, place the milk, cream, sugar and cardamom pods in a saucepan and bring to a simmer. Place the yolks in a bowl and slowly add one-third of the simmering cream while constantly whisking, then gradually add the egg yolks back to the saucepan, again whisking constantly (the same method as for the ice cream).

4. Heat the mixture, stirring constantly, until it reaches a temperature of 183°F. It needs to be just thickened — too little and it will be too thin, but too much... an omelette! A good way to check the consistency is with a back of a spoon: dip it in the custard and then pass your finger across it; if the structure holds, you've got it right.

5. Pass the custard through a fine sieve into a bowl, then to stop the cooking process, dip the bowl in a second bowl of iced water.

6. To make the phyllo tuile, preheat your oven to 400°F. Lay one sheet of phyllo on a baking sheet and brush it with one-third of the melted butter using a pastry brush, then sprinkle with half the granulated sugar and cinnamon.

7. Lay the second phyllo sheet on top and tap it a bit to make the sheets stick together, then repeat step 6. Fold the phyllo sheets in half so that you have 4 layers of phyllo, which means you have one edge that holds all the sheets together, and when cutting you have this edge in every piece of tuile and the layers won't fall apart after baking. If the cutting sounds like too much work, you can always skip the folding procedure and put the phyllo sheets straight in the oven as they are, then after baking, they will be crispy enough for you to easily break into pieces freestyle.

8. Spread the rest of the butter over the top phyllo sheet and scatter with the demerara sugar — this is for added crunch!

9. Cut the stacked sheets into 8 evenly sized pieces and bake for 10–12 minutes until golden brown. Remove from the oven and leave to cool.

10. Make the fig brûlée just before assembling your dish. Cut the figs into quarters, sprinkle the sugar evenly over the cut side of the figs and then caramelize with a blowtorch. If you don't have a blowtorch, grill under a high heat in the oven, careful not to burn, this happens fast!

11. To assemble the dish, spoon the cardamom Anglaise in a circle on 8 plates and crumble some of the tuile in the center (this is to stop the ice cream from moving). Scoop a quenelle of the tahini ice cream (by passing between two spoons) on top, place 3 fig quarters on each plate and decorate with the phyllo tuile — et voilà!

Malabi
See p.206-7

Malabi

Serves 4 (generously)

One of the first desserts I ever made for my family was malabi. This is a rose-scented milk pudding that you will find in every little kiosk or restaurant you pass as you wander the streets of Old Jaffa. It's presented very simply, usually in a plastic container with some desiccated coconut, chopped pistachios and raspberry syrup on top. But don't let the modest exterior fool you — it's one of my most treasured, favorite sweet dishes.

For the restaurant, I wanted to create a modern interpretation of the classic malabi, so every element has received an upgrade. You can either go for the smarter restaurant-style version and serve it in individual ramekins with all the fancy toppings, or do it the family way — one big bowl, a spoon each and everyone digs in. In either case, you can revert to the traditional simple toppings. My heart belongs to both.

---

1. To make the malabi, set aside ½ cup of the milk. Pour the rest into a heavy-bottomed saucepan with the cream and sugar, and simmer, stirring gently, until the sugar has dissolved. Add the cornstarch to the milk you have set aside along with the rose water, and stir until thoroughly blended and there are no lumps of cornstarch left — the best tool to use here is your fingers, as it's the only way to ensure that the malabi has a smooth texture. When the creamy milk boils, give the cornstarch one final stir before adding it to the saucepan of creamy milk. Simmer over a low heat until the mixture begins to thicken, stirring constantly to make sure there are no lumps — this should take no longer than 2 minutes.

2. Once thickened, pour the mixture either into 4 individual ramekins, or a large bowl if you're going family style. Cover with plastic wrap and leave to cool to room temperature, then chill in the fridge for a couple of hours. The malabi can be kept in the fridge for up to 3 days. Now make the toppings.

3. To make the raspberry coulis, stir the raspberries and sugar together in a bain-marie — a heatproof bowl or pan set over a pan of barely simmering water — and cook until soft. This can also be done in a microwave-proof bowl in the microwave on a low heat, but make sure you cover the bowl with plastic wrap so that you don't have a raspberry explosion in your microwave.

4. Pass through a fine sieve or, if you prefer it chunkier, you can leave it as is. The coulis will keep in an airtight container in the fridge for up to 5 days.

5. To make the pistachio brittle, preheat your oven to 350°F. Spread the pistachios out on a baking sheet and toast in the oven for 7 minutes.

6. To make the caramel for the pistachio brittle, heat a heavy-bottomed nonstick pan over a low heat and add the sugar in one even layer. The most important thing here is not to stir — if you're worried about burning, add a couple of drops of water, but otherwise let it be. Once all the sugar has melted and you have a golden caramel, take the pan off the heat, stir in the toasted pistachios and then transfer to a tray lined with

For the malabi
* 2¼ cups milk
* ⅔ cup whipping cream
* ¼ cup granulated sugar
* ⅓ cup cornstarch
* 4 tsp good-quality rose water

For the raspberry coulis
* 1¼ cups raspberries, plus an extra 15–20 to garnish
* ⅓ cup confectioners' sugar

For the pistachio brittle
Can be replaced with ⅓ cup toasted and chopped pistachio nuts — see p.21
* 2 tbsp pistachio nuts
* 3½ tbsp superfine sugar

For the coconut meringue
Can be replaced with 3 tbsp toasted desiccated coconut
* 2 egg whites
* ½ cup granulated sugar
* 2 tbsp water
* ½ cup desiccated coconut

For the crispy kataifi

* ¼ lb kataifi pastry, shredded
  baklava pastry fingers or
  similar
* ¼ cup confectioners' sugar,
  sifted
* ¼ cup unsalted butter, melted
* 2 tbsp rose water

parchment paper. Leave to cool completely, then chop finely. This makes an amazing ice cream topping, too. The pistachio brittle can be kept in an airtight container for up to 2 weeks.

7. To make the coconut meringue, preheat your oven to 275°F and line a baking sheet with parchment paper. Place the egg whites in the bowl of an electric mixer fitted with a whisk attachment and beat to soft peaks.

8. Put 2 tablespoons water and the sugar in a saucepan and heat until you have a syrup that reaches 250°F in temperature, then pour into the egg whites in a slow, steady stream while beating on a high speed. Once combined, spoon the mixture into a piping bag fitted with a ½-inch plain piping nozzle.

9. Scatter the desiccated coconut in an even layer on a tray. Now pipe ½-inch spheres of the meringue mixture on to the tray, then roll the balls to coat them in the lovely coconut shards. Transfer the coconut balls to the lined baking sheet and bake for 1½ hours until nice and dry (every oven is different from one another, so you may need another 30 minutes, but just make sure the meringues are completely dry). You'll have rather more meringues than you need here, but whisking a smaller quantity of egg whites is tricky, and besides, you're going to be nibbling them anyway — or you can use them as a fairly unbeatable ice cream topping. The meringues will keep in an airtight container for up to 2 weeks.

10. To make the crispy kataifi, preheat your oven to 400°F. Using your fingers, crumble the kataifi into a mixing bowl, add the confectioners' sugar and mix to coat well. Pour in the melted butter and rose water and mix again.

11. Spread the mixture on to a baking sheet and bake for 12–15 minutes until it's turned a lovely golden color and is nice and crispy. The nibbling risk factor is high with this, too, so I'd recommend you make in double or triple quantities.

12. To assemble the dish, grab your malabi from the fridge, pour over some of the raspberry coulis, scatter your toppings at whim, top with the extra raspberries and enjoy the explosion of flavors and textures.

For the simple syrup

* ¾ cup granulated sugar
* ⅔ cup water
* 1 star anise
* 1 cardamom pod
* 1 clove

For the orange syrup

* ½ cup granulated sugar
* ⅔ cup orange juice
* 1 star anise
* 1 cardamom pod
* 1 clove

Basbousa

Semolina cake with kumquat jam & whipped yogurt
Serves 10

This was the first cake ever to be baked at Machneyuda in Jerusalem, and the first cake I learned how to make as a new chef at the restaurant. That was also the day I met Shablool, who was to be my co-pastry chef. Put simply, we are complete opposites, and at the beginning we used to fight and argue about every little thing. But as time went by, we came to love each other with all our flaws, just like real family. Even now we talk nearly every day and advise each other when we're about to put something new on the menu. His real name is Moses, but chef Uri gave him the ironic nickname Shablool, meaning "snail" in Hebrew. He's one of the fastest pastry chefs I know.

The recipe for this excellent moist, flavorful semolina cake, usually served at teatime, was given to me by Shablool, and given to him, in turn, by Irit Navon — Uri's mama. I follow her original recipe (if it ain't broke…), which is great on its own, but if you feel like going the extra mile, I've included recipes for the jam and whipped yogurt we serve it with at the restaurant.

The word basbousa, *by the way, translates as "stop kissing" (*bas = *"stop," *bousa = *"kiss") — meaning "You're too sweet!"*

---

1. Start with the simple syrup so that it will have time to chill before you need it. Boil all ingredients together in a saucepan until the sugar has completely dissolved. Leave to cool, then cover and refrigerate with the spices still in it so that you get the maximum flavor from them. The syrup will keep in the fridge for up to a month in a sterilized airtight bottle or jar (see p.24).

2. To make the orange syrup, bring all the ingredients to the boil in a saucepan, then lower the heat and simmer until reduced by half. Leave to cool. The syrup can be kept in the fridge for up to a week in a sterilized airtight container (see p.24).

3. To make the cake, preheat your oven to 400°F and line a cake pan about 10¾ x 12¾ inches with parchment paper.

4. Mix all the dry ingredients together in a mixing bowl with a whisk.

5. Beat the egg yolks with the orange juice, then mix into the dry ingredients until combined. Add the melted butter slowly, whisking constantly.

6. In a separate bowl, whisk the egg whites to soft peaks, then gently fold into the cake mixture. Pour the cake mixture into the lined pan and bake for 30 minutes on the middle shelf of the oven.

7. Remove the cake from the oven and immediately pour the chilled simple syrup, strained of its spices, over it. It's very important that the cake is hot and the syrup is cold (I love the sizzling sound this makes — that's when you know you've got the temperatures right), as the cake will then absorb the syrup much better and you'll get

→ **Ingredients and recipe continued on next page**

a nice moist crumb. This principle applies to all baked goods that are soaked in syrup. Leave the cake to cool in the pan, then cut into squares.

8. To make the kumquat jam, cut the kumquats in half and remove the seeds — make sure none of them remain, otherwise the jam will be bitter.

9. Place the kumquats in a large pan, cover with water and bring to a boil. Cook for 3 minutes, then drain and put the kumquats in a bowl of iced water to stop the cooking process. Repeat this process twice more, which may sound like a hassle but it's very important not to be lazy and skip this bit, because otherwise you'll end up with bitter jam and only yourself to blame!

10. Place the blanched kumquats with the rest of the ingredients in a large pan — the jam has a tendency to rise when it's simmering, so it's better to be on the safe side and go for ample capacity. Cook over a medium heat until the mixture boils and all the sugar has dissolved.

11. Reduce the heat and simmer for another 30–40 minutes — the kumquats should look transparent. If any of the seeds have found their way in, this is when you will spot them and can remove.

12. Let the jam cool, then transfer to a sterilized airtight jar or container (see p.24) and store in the fridge, where it will keep for up to a month.

13. To make the whipped yogurt, whisk all the ingredients together in a mixing bowl to stiff peaks. The yogurt can be kept in the fridge, tightly covered with plastic wrap or in a container, for up to 3 days.

14. I like to serve the cake warm, either straight after pouring over the sugar syrup, or warmed for a few seconds in a microwave. The best way is to serve it family style and put the jam, orange syrup and yogurt in serving bowls and let everyone help themselves.

For the cake

* 1 cup semolina flour
* 1 cup all-purpose flour
* ½ cup granulated sugar
* ½ cup desiccated coconut
* 2 tsp baking powder
* 5 eggs, separated
* ¾ cup orange juice
* ⅔ cup butter, melted

For the kumquat jam

* 1lb kumquats
* 2 cups granulated sugar
* 4 tbsp water
* 1 star anise
* 2 cardamom pods
* 2 cloves

For the whipped yogurt

* 1¼ cups heavy cream
* ⅔ cup Greek yogurt
* ½ cup confectioners' sugar, sifted

* ½ cup hot water
* ½ tsp Earl Grey, or 2 tea bags
* 2 eggs
* ½ cup vegetable oil
* ⅓ cup runny honey, plus extra to serve
* ½ cup turbinado sugar
* 1⅓ cups all-purpose flour
* 1 tsp baking powder
* ½ tsp baking soda
* 1 scant tsp ground cinnamon
* 2 tsp finely chopped thyme
* grated zest of 1 unwaxed orange
* ½ cup walnuts, roughly chopped

Honey cake

Serves 12

We have many customs to set off Rosh Hashanah, the Jewish New Year, in festive style. A lot of them revolve around food (surprise, surprise), and we eat certain things to symbolize the way we wish our year ahead to be. My personal favorites are all the honey-based sweets, and traditionally we eat these so that sweetness will follow us all year round. And why argue with tradition? This recipe produces a lovely moist cake, and to make it a little more interesting I've added thyme and orange zest, which might sound unusual but tastes wonderful and gives it something extra. It's a really easy recipe to make, all in one bowl, and the end result is an aromatic, moreish cake.

1. Preheat your oven to 350°F and line a 2lb loaf pan with parchment paper.

2. Pour the hot water over the tea and leave the flavors to infuse, or in other words, make a really strong cup of tea. Let cool.

3. Beat the eggs, oil, honey and sugar together in a mixing bowl using a whisk. Add the rest of the ingredients except the walnuts and mix just until it all comes together.

4. Strain the tea, add it to the cake mixture and mix until combined — the batter will be very liquid at this point, but that's fine.

5. Pour the batter into the lined pan and sprinkle with the walnuts — don't worry if some sink in. Bake for 40 minutes or until the cake passes the skewer test: insert a cocktail stick into the center of the cake, and if it comes out with wet batter on it, the cake needs a bit more baking time, but if it comes out clean, then it's ready. Transfer to a wire rack and leave to cool. Serve with extra runny honey.

Stilton cheesecake

Serves 12

One day Zoe came to me with a special request — a cheese course, but not the predictable cheese and biscuits. Not that there's anything wrong with that, but this had to be special. As a sworn cheese fan myself, I was happy to take on the challenge.

I have to admit that this cheesecake isn't for everyone — it's definitely for the more adventurous dessert eaters out there. The dish is a bit of a roller coaster of flavors and textures, combining savory, sweet, spicy, crunchy and smooth all at the same time. The cake itself is very easy to make. If you're in a hurry you can simply serve it with a variety of fruits. But if you want to go the whole hog (and trust me you do), I've included recipes for an accompanying coulis and tuile, just as we serve it in the restaurant. The tuile makes the perfect snack on its own, so I would definitely recommend making a few more of these while you're at it — after all, it's hard not to pinch a tuile or three along the way.

---

1. To make the cheesecake, preheat your oven to 350°F and line a 1½ lb loaf pan with parchment paper.

2. Mix all the ingredients together in a mixing bowl, then pour the mixture into the lined tin. Bake for 25–30 minutes until it is firm but with a slight wobble when you shake it gently — a bit like a jelly. Place in the fridge until completely cool, then it's ready to cut and serve. It will keep in the fridge for up to 3 days.

3. To make the apricot coulis, place all the ingredients in a saucepan and cook over a medium heat for about 20 minutes until the apricots have softened.

4. Transfer to a blender and blend until smooth, then pass through a fine sieve for an ultra-smooth texture. The coulis will keep in an airtight container in the fridge for up to 4 days.

5. To make the pumpkin seed tuile, preheat your oven to 375°F.

6. Place the sugar, corn syrup, butter and milk in a heavy-bottomed saucepan and heat to 230°F. Remove the pan from the heat, add the pumpkin seeds and cornstarch and mix to combine.

7. Using a rolling pin, roll the mixture out into a thin layer between 2 sheets of parchment paper. Do this while the mixture is still hot, otherwise it will start to set and will be hard to roll thinly. Remove the top sheet of parchment paper, then transfer the flattened tuile mixture, still on the bottom sheet of parchment paper, to a baking sheet. Scatter the tuile with the crushed red pepper flakes and bake for 12 minutes until it is an amber caramel color.

8. Remove from the oven and leave to cool completely. Break the tuile up into pieces and transfer to an airtight container, where it will keep for up to 2 weeks.

9. To serve, cut the cake into 12 equal-sized pieces. Place a teaspoon of the apricot coulis on each serving plate and top with a piece of the cake and a piece of tuile.

For the cake

* 1½ cups full-fat soft cheese
* ⅓ cup honey
* 1 egg
* 1 tbsp blue Stilton cheese, crumbled
* 1 tsp salt

For the apricot coulis

* ⅔ cup apricots (3–4), pitted
* ¼ cup granulated sugar
* 1 tbsp water

For the pumpkin seed tuile

* 3 tbsp granulated sugar
* 2 tsp corn syrup
* 2 tbsp butter
* 2 tsp milk
* ⅓ cup pumpkin seeds
* 1 tsp cornstarch
* 2–3 pinches of crushed red pepper flakes

For the filling

* 2¼ cups pitted dates
  (I like to use Medjool because
  they're plump and sweet),
  roughly chopped
* 3 tbsp vegetable oil
* 3 tbsp water
* 1 tsp ground cardamom or
  finely grated unwaxed orange
  zest (optional)

For the dough

* 2 cups all-purpose flour, plus
  extra for dusting if needed
* 1 tsp baking powder
* pinch of salt
* 2½ tbsp granulated sugar
* 6 tbsp very soft butter (but not
  melted)
* ¼ cup vegetable oil
* ¼ cup milk
* 1 tsp vanilla extract
* confectioners' sugar, for
  dusting

Date roulade

Or ma'amul for the lazy

Makes 20–30

I really like ma'amul cookies, which consist of crumbly pastry filled with date paste. They are seriously yummy, but involve a lot of work; each one must be filled individually, and they're usually finished with a special pattern. The trick to this lazy version is to make a filled roulade and simply cut it into loads of cookies — ma'amul in half the time.

This is not actually my recipe but my beloved older sister Yasmin's, and every time I make these I remember the first time she made them for me. It was a sunny day, so I decided to take a shortcut through the park on the way over to her house. The weather turned on me very quickly: it was suddenly dark and rainy (yes, it does rain in Israel!) and my leisurely stroll turned into a muddy dash. I arrived soaked to the bone and immediately ran for a change of clothes. When I returned to the living room, waiting for me was a pot of mint tea and a pile of ma'amul cookies.

1. Preheat your oven to 375°F and line a baking sheet with parchment paper.

2. To make the filling, put all the ingredients in a blender and blend until you have a smooth texture with no visible date skin.

3. To make the dough, mix all the dough ingredients together in a mixing bowl until they have all combined to a soft and slightly sticky dough. There's no need to use an electric mixer — it's very easy to do by hand. The mixture will start off looking too wet, but keep kneading and the dough will absorb all the liquid.

4. Roll out the dough between 2 pieces of parchment paper to a thin rectangle about 10 inches x 16 inches in size, and ⅛ inch thick — dust the paper with flour if it sticks.

5. Take off the top sheet of parchment paper and spread the filling on to the dough. If it gets too sticky, dip your spoon in water from time to time. Starting from the one long side, roll the dough into a roulade, using the parchment paper to help you roll. Then simply lift the parchment paper and separate the dough from it, and roll the dough a little more to seal the seam underneath the roulade.

6. Transfer the roulade to the lined baking sheet. Score it at ⅝-inch intervals using a sharp knife — this will make it easier to cut the roulade after baking. Bake for 30–40 minutes until golden brown.

7. Remove from the oven and let cool for about 15 minutes. Then dust with confectioners' sugar and slice the roulade where you marked it before baking.

Reverse Earl Grey chocolate fondue

Serves 8

It's time for you to meet my lovely sous pastry chef Kader, aka Junior, so called because he was the youngest chef in our kitchen when he started out and actually began working at The Palomar as a kitchen porter. A few months after the restaurant opened I was still working in the pastry kitchen all by myself, and it was clear that I needed some help, so Tomer suggested some of the younger chefs, but I insisted on Junior because he is a bright young man with kind eyes, and something inside me just knew that he would make a great chef.

So back to the story behind this recipe, which, like many other very good recipes, was born by mistake. It was Junior's second week in the pastry kitchen, and he was learning and progressing very fast, so I decided to trust him to work alone for a few hours while I did some boring office work. The next day, when he was about to roll the truffles from the recipe he had made the day before, he turned to me with anxious, guilty eyes and confessed, "Chef, there's something wrong." He had apparently added too much milk to the truffle mixture so it hadn't set. To try and fix it, I warmed it up and melted the chocolate — then wow! The texture was wonderful; liquid yet rich and creamy, just like a fondue. The timing couldn't have been better as it happened to be Valentine's Day! I wanted to put it on the menu the same day, but we didn't have any fondue sticks. So we reversed the concept, and instead of dipping treats into the fondue, we served them all on the plate and poured the fondue sauce on top.

As with all my recipes, you can have fun creating all the treats for dipping or you can keep it simple — a few strawberries and some marshmallows will do a magnificent job.

---

1. To make the Earl Grey fondue, bring the milk, cream and Earl Grey tea to a boil in a saucepan. Take off the heat, cover with plastic wrap and leave to infuse for 10 minutes so that the milk mixture takes on all the flavor from the tea.
2. Meanwhile, melt the chocolate in a heatproof bowl set over a pan of barely simmering water, or in the microwave on a low heat, making sure you stir it at frequent intervals so that it doesn't burn.
3. Back to the milk — remove the tea bags from the milk and squeeze them out into the milk to extract all the flavor, or strain and press out the tea leaves. For the next step the milk needs to be fairly warm, so if it has cooled down too much, reheat it just a little.
4. Pour the warm milk into the melted chocolate and mix using a whisk until well combined, then whisk in the butter. You can keep the fondue mixture in the fridge, tightly covered in plastic wrap, until ready to warm up for serving.

For the Earl Grey fondue
* 7 tbsp milk
* 7 tbsp whipping cream
* 2 Earl Gray tea bags or 2 heaping tsp loose Earl Gray tea
* ¾ cup milk chocolate, broken into pieces
* ¾ tbsp butter

→ **Ingredients and recipe continued on the next page**

5. For the whisky pears, bring the ¾ cup water and the sugar to a boil in a saucepan. Add the pears and whisky and cook for about 10 minutes until the pears have softened but are still firm, turning the cubes halfway through so that they cook evenly. Check if they're ready by inserting a knife into one of the pieces — if it goes in easily, it means they're ready, but if you need to use force, they need a bit more cooking.

6. Remove from the heat and leave the pears to cool in the syrup. Then cover and store them in the fridge, still in the syrup — not only will they keep for longer (up to 1 week), but they will also develop in flavor.

7. To make the cardamom marshmallow, boil the water, sugar, glucose and inverted syrup together in a saucepan until you have a syrup that reaches 250°F in temperature. Transfer to the bowl of an electric mixer fitted with a whisk attachment and leave to cool to 212°F.

8. Add the squeezed-out gelatin and cardamom and whisk for about 5–6 minutes on a high speed until the mixture starts to stick to the sides of the bowl and form strands.

9. This is the tricky part. The marshmallow mixture is probably the stickiest thing you'll ever touch, so what we do to mitigate against sticky hell is to oil everything it will come into contact with, meaning your spatula and the container it's going in, which should measure about 6 inches x 10 inches. And to be on the safe side, line the container with parchment paper and brush that with oil, too.

10. Now that everything is oiled, it's safe to transfer the marshmallow mixture to the container. If it's sticking, just brush with more oil. Cover with another sheet of oiled parchment paper and flatten the surface evenly. Set aside in a cool place (but not the fridge) for at least 3 hours to firm up. To see if it's ready, give it a poke — you're looking for a bouncy texture.

11. Mix the cornstarch and confectioners' sugar together in a bowl for dusting the marshmallow to help with cutting it up, since it'll still be sticky. Dust a chopping board with the cornstarch mixture. Peel the parchment paper from the marshmallow and tip it onto the board. Start cutting it into cubes, and keep dusting as you go so that every marshmallow cube is coated in the cornstarch mixture to prevent them from sticking to each other. If necessary, toss the cubes a little in your hands to remove any excess cornstarch mixture. You can store the marshmallow in an airtight container at room temperature for up to a month.

12. For the croutons, preheat your oven to 400°F and line a baking sheet with parchment paper. Spread the bread cubes out on the lined baking sheet and dust lightly with confectioners' sugar. Bake for about 8–10 minutes until golden brown. Remove from the oven and leave to cool. Keep the oven on.

13. For the sumac crumble, ensure the oven is still set to 400°F and line a baking sheet with parchment paper.

14. Mix the butter with the sugar, then rub into the rest of the ingredients until it resembles bread crumbs. Spread out the crumble mixture on to the lined tray and bake for 30 minutes or until golden brown, mixing every 10 minutes to prevent it from burning. Remove from the oven and let cool.

For the whisky pears

* ¾ cup water
* ½ cup granulated sugar
* 4 pears, peeled, cored and cut into ¾-inch cubes
* 4 tsp whisky

For the cardamom marshmallow

* 2½ tbsp water
* ⅔ cup granulated sugar
* ¼ cup glucose
* 2¼ tbsp inverted sugar syrup
* ¾ tsp gelatin, soaked according to the package instructions
* ½ tsp ground cardamom
* vegetable oil, for oiling
* ¾ cup cornstarch
* 1 cup confectioners' sugar, sifted

For the croutons

* 1 Kubaneh Bread (see p.230) or 3 slices of Challah (see p.238) or brioche, cut into ½-inch cubes
* confectioners' sugar, for dusting

For the sumac crumble

* * ½ cup cold butter,
  cut into cubes
* * ¾ cup all-purpose flour
* * ½ cup granulated sugar
* * ¾ cup ground almonds
* * 3 tbsp sumac

15. Place in a food processor and blend in 2–3 brief pulses until coarsely ground, or chop by hand if you prefer it in big chunks. The crumble can be stored in an airtight container for up to 2 weeks.

16. To serve, reheat the fondue if necessary. You can do this in the microwave on a low heat, mixing every 10 seconds, or in a heatproof bowl set over a pan of simmering water, stirring occasionally, until it is runny and warm.

17. Place a thin layer of the crumble in the base of a serving dish. Arrange the pears, marshmallow and croutons over the top of the crumble so that each bite will give you a different treat. Finally, pour the warm fondue over the dish in front of your guests.

Jerusalem mess

Serves 4

Many guests at our restaurant have told me that this dessert brings an upmarket version of Eton Mess to mind. It's easy to see why, as it features the familiar cream, strawberries and meringue. So when we tried to come up with a name, the various suggestions included The Palomar's Eton Mess, Strawberries and Labneh, and Messy Garden! But none of these felt right. My inspiration instead was a childhood dessert that my mum used to make — sour cream with sugar and strawberries (Mama's Mess, if you like!) — and I wanted its name to reflect those origins, too. It's Eton Mess but Jerusalem style.

For the labneh cream

* 1¼ cups heavy cream
* ½ cup granulated sugar
* ¾ cup Labneh (see p.41)

For the almond crumble

* ½ cup cold butter,
  cut into cubes
* ½ cup granulated sugar
* ¾ cup all-purpose flour
* 1 cup ground almonds
* ½ tsp vanilla extract

For the apple jelly

* ½ cup unsweetened apple juice
* 4 tsp elderflower cordial
* ¾ tsp gelatin, soaked according
  to the package instructions

For the strawberry coulis

* ¾ cup strawberries, hulled and
  chopped
* 2 tbsp granulated sugar
* 1 tbsp water

→ Ingredients and recipe
continued on the next page

1. To make the labneh cream, whip the cream and sugar together in a mixing bowl to soft peaks.

2. Place the labneh in a separate mixing bowl and gently fold in the whipped cream. This can be kept in the fridge, tightly covered with plastic wrap, for up to 4 days.

3. To make the almond crumble, preheat the oven to 400°F and line a baking sheet with parchment paper.

4. Mix the butter with the sugar, then rub into the rest of the ingredients until it resembles bread crumbs. Spread out the crumble mixture on to the lined baking sheet and bake for 20–30 minutes or until golden brown, mixing every 10 minutes to prevent it from burning. Remove from the oven and leave to cool.

5. Place in a food processor and blend in 2–3 brief pulses until coarsely ground, or chop by hand if you prefer it in big chunks. The crumble can be stored in an airtight container for up to 2 weeks.

6. To make the apple jelly, warm up the apple juice and elderflower in a pan until it is almost boiling. But don't let it boil, otherwise it will lose some of its flavor.

7. Squeeze the excess water from the gelatine and add it to the pan, then stir until it has dissolved. Pour the mixture into a small rectangular container about 3¼ inches x 6 inches in size — the jelly needs to be about ½–⅝ inch thick. Leave the jelly to set in the fridge for at least 2 hours.

8. When completely set, transfer the jelly from the container to a chopping board — run a knife around the edges to loosen it if necessary. Cut into ½–⅝ inch evenly sized cubes and place in an airtight container. If you have more than one layer, separate the layers with parchment paper so that they won't stick to one another. The jelly will keep in the fridge for up to 4 days.

9. To make the strawberry coulis, place the berries in a pan with the sugar and the water and cook gently until they have softened. Blend in a blender or food processor until smooth, then pass through a fine sieve — or not if you prefer a chunky coulis. It will keep in an airtight container in the fridge for up to 4 days.

10. To make the lemon curd, mix all the ingredients together in a heatproof bowl using a whisk until just combined. Set the bowl over a pan of barely simmering water (make sure the bowl doesn't touch the water) and cook, stirring frequently, until the mixture thickens to a curd consistency.

11. Pass the curd through a fine sieve. Don't skip this part, as it strains out any egg that has been cooked during the heating process, otherwise you'll end up with a sour omelet!

12. Remove the bowl from the pan of water and leave the curd to cool slightly, or to 100°F if you want to be precise. It's easy to check the temperature even without a thermometer, since it's almost the same as body temperature. If you've checked a baby's milk bottle before, this will be easy for you; if not, stick your finger in the mixture, and if it feels hot, then it's still too hot. Be patient and let it cool down properly, then blend in a blender or food processor until the butter is combined. If the curd feels cold, then it's cooled too much, in which case blend it anyway (the risk of warming it up again and cooking the egg is too high). It will have more of a buttery taste if blended when cooler, but will still be very good. The curd will keep in the fridge in an airtight container for up to 3 days.

13. To make the meringue, preheat your oven to 250°F and line a baking sheet with parchment paper. Place the egg white in the bowl of an electric mixer fitted with a whisk attachment and beat to soft peaks.

14. Boil the water and sugar together in a saucepan until you have a syrup that reaches 250°F in temperature, then pour into the egg white in a slow, steady stream while beating on a high speed. Continue beating until the mixture is shiny and fluffy, yet stable.

15. Spread a thin even layer of the meringue mixture over the lined baking sheet and sprinkle the wafer bits evenly over the top. Bake for about 1 hour or until dry and crisp. The meringue will not change in color, but the way to check whether it's ready or not is to break a piece — if it breaks easily, it's ready, but if it bends instead of breaking, then it needs more cooking time. Let cool completely, then store in an airtight container for up to a month at room temperature.

16. To serve, scatter the almond crumble over the serving plates, then pipe the labneh cream on top or shape into quenelles by passing between 2 spoons. Scatter a little of each of the other ingredients on each plate so that your guests will get a taste of everything in each bite. This way of serving is only a suggestion — you can obviously simply throw everything in a bowl and dig in!

For the lemon curd
* 5 tbsp freshly squeezed lemon juice
* ½ cup granulated sugar
* 1 egg
* 2 egg yolks
* ¼ cup cold butter, cut into cubes

For the meringue
* 2 tbsp egg white (about 1 egg)
* 1 tbsp water
* ⅓ cup granulated sugar
* 3 tbsp wafer crumbs

To serve
* handful of strawberries, cut into quarters
* small handful of micro basil (optional)
* small handful of micro sorrel (optional)

Lion's Milk
See cocktail insert for recipe

Pita bread

Makes 14 mini or 10 large pita breads

* 4 cups all-purpose flour, plus extra for dusting
* 2 tbsp fresh yeast (or 2¼ tsp fast-acting dried yeast)
* 1 tbsp granulated sugar
* ½ tbsp salt
* 1½ cups cold water
* 3 tbsp canola or vegetable oil

I have a confession to make: the first time I ever baked pita breads was only after I moved to the UK. In Jerusalem I used to live in the Machane Yehuda market above a very famous pita bakery (not helpful for one's figure!), but even if I hadn't lived there, really good pita is so easy to come by; you can get it everywhere. When we moved to the UK to open The Palomar, I just couldn't find the pita I loved, so I did the only reasonable thing in the circumstances and started to bake it myself. I can't tell you how exciting it was the first time they popped up in the oven. It was hypnotic, sitting there watching them. And then, like magic, poof! That is what's so fun about pita bread — if it puffs up well, it offers the perfect pocket for filling, so it is great for sandwiches, and of course ideal for the national Israeli sport of scooping hummus!

1. In the bowl of an electric mixer fitted with a dough hook, or in a mixing bowl if making by hand, mix all the dry ingredients together, then mix in the water and oil.

2. Knead on a low speed for about 10 minutes, or by hand in a bowl, until elastic — we need to develop the gluten enough to allow the pita to pop.

3. Cover with a clean dish towel and let rise at room temperature for 30 minutes or until doubled in size (it might take a bit longer if your room is cold).

4. Flour your work surface, transfer the dough to it and divide into either 14 pieces of about 2¼oz each (for mini pitas) or 10 pieces of about 3oz each (for large pitas).

5. Roll each piece of dough into a ball. We're now going to let the balls proof, so arrange them on the floured work surface with a ¾–1¼ inch space between each ball. Cover with the dish towel and leave for 10–15 minutes — the balls should double in size in this time. Meanwhile, preheat your oven to 475°F — the intense heat evaporates the liquid in the dough, creating steam that will separate the 2 walls, which is what makes the pita pop!

6. Still on the floured work surface, use a rolling pin to flatten the balls into 4½-inch rounds for mini pitas or 6¼-inch rounds for large pitas. It's very important that they are of an equal thickness for them all to pop correctly.

7. Arrange the rolled-out pitas on 2 large baking sheets, each lined with parchment paper, and set aside to rest for another 10–15 minutes.

8. Bake for 8–10 minutes. Once the pitas pop up (see photo opposite), you know they're baked on the inside, so you can just give them an extra 1–2 minutes to color.

9. The moment the pitas come out of the oven, place in a container and cover with a clean dish towel or put into a plastic bag and seal until they cool down. This will allow the pitas to soften.

Kubaneh bread

Makes 6 small loaves or 3 larger loaves

Kubaneh is a traditional Yemeni bread, traditionally baked overnight in a special lidded aluminium pot. According to Orthodox Jewish law, you're not permitted to cook from sunset on Friday to sunset the following day, so this lovely bread was born out of necessity, which in turn became a ritual. The end result is beautifully rich in texture.

I first encountered kubaneh bread on my military service in Israel when I went to stay with a friend one weekend (so that I wouldn't be too far away from the base) whose grandma was an expert in traditional Yemeni cuisine. I'd experimented with bread making once or twice before, but I had never seen anyone dipping their hands in melted butter and thinly spreading it over the dough. This was exciting! Even more exciting was waking up early the next morning to the heavenly smell of buttery fresh bread, running down to the kitchen to lift the lid of the pot and tasting kubaneh for the first time.

When we opened The Palomar, we knew we needed a bread that was perfectly suited to plate-mopping, so I came up with this fluffy version of kubaneh. Luckily for us (and you), it needs only 30 minutes' baking. You don't need special baking proficiency to make this bread — just be fearless!

As kubaneh baking pots are not something to be found in every home, you can use 4½-inch baking rings instead to make individual loaves, or 2 lb loaf pans, each measuring 11 x 5 inches for larger ones.

---

* 4 cups all-purpose flour, plus extra for dusting if making by hand
* 2 tbsp fresh yeast (or 2¼ tsp active dry yeast)
* ¾ tbsp salt
* ⅓ cup granulated sugar
* 1 small egg
* 1⅓ cups cold water
* ½ cup unsalted butter

1. In the bowl of an electric mixer fitted with a dough hook, or in a mixing bowl if making by hand, mix the flour and yeast together on a low speed, then add the salt and the sugar. Mix in the egg and the water, making sure there is no flour left unmixed at the base of the bowl. The dough will be very sticky, but do not worry — this is exactly how it should be, so do not be tempted to add any flour.

2. Knead the dough on a low speed for 3 minutes, or by hand in a bowl, then cover the bowl with plastic wrap and leave the dough to rest for 10 minutes.

3. Uncover the dough and knead it for about 1 minute to let some of the air out, then re-cover with plastic wrap and leave to rest for another 10 minutes. Repeat this kneading and resting process, then uncover and knead once more to let the air out — three times in total.

4. Leave the dough to rise for about an hour or until tripled in size.

5. Next comes the fun part — it's time for some hand-in-butter action. Line a large baking sheet with parchment paper. Take 4½-inch baking rings (if going that route) and place on the baking sheet. Melt the butter in a pan on the burner or in the microwave — it should be lukewarm rather than piping-hot, otherwise dipping your hands in it will be no fun at all.

6. Clean your work surface and use your hands to grease it with a little of the melted butter. Make sure you keep your hands and work surface nicely buttered throughout.

Now divide the dough into 6 evenly sized balls. Take the first ball and, using your buttered hands, begin to spread the dough into a thin sheet roughly 12 x 16½ inches — it's OK if you get a hole here and there. Keep buttering your hands and work surface if needed.

7. Use your hands to roll the sheet into a tight tube. Now spiral the tube into a coil and place in a baking ring. Repeat with the rest of the balls of dough. If using loaf tins, you can fit three balls of dough in one tin.

8. Once your baking sheet is loaded with the 6 beautiful kubaneh coils, leave them to proof for 30 minutes or until tripled in size. Meanwhile, preheat your oven to 400°F.

9. Bake the kubaneh for 20–25 minutes (or 30 minutes if using loaf tins), turning the baking sheet around halfway through cooking to ensure a nice even color on each loaf.

10. Take the baking sheet out of the oven and leave the loaves to cool for 10 minutes (I warn you, that'll be a tough 10 minutes — the smell will drive you mad). Now remove from the rings and that's it — you are ready to rip and dip! In the restaurant we serve the kubaneh with our White Tahini Sauce (see p.28) and Velvet Tomatoes (see p.30), but any kind of sauce, mezze or salad is up to task. To keep the loaves fresh, make sure they're kept tightly wrapped or sealed and they'll be fine overnight at room temperature, or for up to 3 days in the fridge. Or follow our mothers' example and freeze a couple so that you're always at the ready for an unexpected guest. They defrost brilliantly, and are very easy to warm up.

Fricassee

Makes 24 mini balls or 4 buns

Who doesn't like fried dough? Fricassee is basically a Tunisian-style doughnut, except that the Tunisians use it as a bun for a savory filling, which provided the inspiration for our Cured Mackerel Fricassee recipe (see p.92). As the dough flavor is versatile, you can fill it with whatever comes to mind and go sweet as well as savory. I like to use the bigger version in the more classic way to make a sandwich. The smaller mini balls can easily become a sweet nibble — all you need to do is dust them with confectioners' sugar as soon as they come out of the hot oil.

* 1 cup all-purpose flour, plus extra for dusting
* 1 tsp fresh yeast (or pinch of active dry yeast)
* 1 tsp sugar
* 6 tbsp warm water
* 2 tsp canola oil, plus 4¼ cups for deep-frying

1. Mix all the ingredients (except the oil for deep-frying) together in a mixing bowl until well combined — this recipe is so small that there's no need to use an electric mixer. You will have a very sticky dough but that's okay, as the stickier it is, the fluffier the end result, so don't be tempted to add more flour.

2. Cover the bowl with plastic wrap and leave to rise at room temperature for 20 minutes or until doubled in size.

3. On a floured work surface, shape the dough into balls or elongate into buns: ¾ tbsp of dough for each mini ball or 5 tbsp for each bun. If it's easier for you, simply divide the dough into the number of pieces you want, i.e. 24 mini balls or 4 buns. Place on a floured tray and leave to rest (uncovered) for another 10–15 minutes.

4. Heat the oil for deep-frying in a deep saucepan to 375°F. Gently transfer the dough balls or buns from the tray to the oil, trying not to let the air out, and deep-fry — the mini balls in small batches or the buns two at a time — until golden on both sides. Remove from the oil and drain on paper towels. The fricassee must be eaten on the same day, as like all fried dough they won't taste as good if kept any longer.

* 2 cups all-purpose flour
* ¼ cup softened butter
* 2 tsp fresh yeast (or 1¼ tsp fast-acting dry yeast)
* 1 tsp mahlab (see p.18)
* 5 tbsp canola oil
* 1½ tsp salt
* ½ cup warm water
* 1 egg, beaten, for egg wash
* sesame seeds, for scattering

Abadi-style savory cookies

Makes 50–55 cookies

These addictive savory cookies are usually eaten in my house at teatime — one thing the Moroccans and English share is a love of tea. After every big meal my mama always brings out a big pot of mint tea and a big plate of these great cookies. The secret to the awesome flavor is in the mahlab spice made from cherry pits, which is bitter when raw but, once it's baked, you can't resist that smell. If you don't have mahlab in your pantry, these cookies are super tasty even without. When we bake these cookies at the restaurant, we make sure we seal and store them as soon as they've cooled down, as the smell brings the staff to the trays and before I know it I need to bake a second batch. As I said, addictive!

1. In the bowl of an electric mixer fitted with the paddle attachment, mix the flour, butter, yeast and mahlab together until the mixture resembles bread crumbs.

2. Add oil and salt and mix for a few seconds — we still want a crumbly texture, so don't overmix.

3. Add the warm water and mix for a few minutes until you get a sticky dough — the dough will come away from the sides of the bowl. Set aside and let rest for 30 minutes.

4. Preheat your oven to 375°F and line a couple of baking sheets with parchment paper. To shape each cookie, take a small amount of dough, about 1 inch in diameter, and rub it between your hands to elongate it and create a strip about 4½ inches long and about ¼ inch thick. If it gets sticky just oil your hands a little bit. At that point, you can either leave the dough as a strip or form it into a ring shape and press the ends together to seal.

5. Place the dough shapes on the lined baking sheets, brush with the egg wash and scatter with sesame seeds. Bake for 25–30 minutes until golden and crisp. Leave the cookies to cool, then stow away immediately, or just start on a second batch!

Challah

Makes 1 loaf

Challah is a traditional enriched bread made for Friday night dinner and holidays, and since it's only on sale at the weekend, it has a very special status. At Friday night dinner, it's a Jewish tradition to say a blessing for the challah bread before tearing it, dipping it in salt and devouring it. Once when I asked my grandpa why we do this, he told me that it's to remember that a meal without bread is not a meal and that there's no flavor to life without salt. I don't think Grandpa was citing the Bible here, but I always loved his poetic take on things.

In my family, we eat challah with almost every weekend meal, whether dipped in the sauce of a Friday night stew or as French toast on Saturday morning. The most treasured tradition in my house is "sandwiching" and challah is the perfect bread for the job. It has a way of transforming the simplest sandwich into a fancy one. My mum would often make a sabich sandwich, filled with fried eggplant, tahini and hard-boiled egg seasoned with salt and cumin. The tahini and oil from the eggplant form a delicious sauce and the challah soaks it all up — it really hits the spot.

* 4 cups strong white bread flour, plus extra for dusting
* 2 tbsp fresh yeast, crumbled so that it's evenly distributed in the dough (or 2¼ tsp fast-acting dried yeast)
* ¼ cup turbinado sugar
* ¼ cup vegetable oil, plus extra for oiling and brushing
* 1 small egg, plus extra, beaten, for egg wash
* salt
* ¾ cup water
* sesame seeds, for scattering

1. Combine all the ingredients (except the sesame seeds) in the bowl of an electric mixer fitted with a dough hook (or in a mixing bowl if making by hand, if you have the upper-body strength!) and knead on a low speed for 7–10 minutes until you have a smooth but slightly sticky dough.

2. Transfer the dough to a lightly oiled bowl and brush the surface of the dough with oil to prevent it drying out. Cover with a clean dish towel and leave to rise at room temperature for about an hour or until doubled in size. Meanwhile, line a baking sheet with parchment paper.

3. Divide the dough into thirds. On a lightly floured work surface, take one piece of dough and flatten slightly with your hands to create a small rectangle, then roll it up, starting from one longer side, and continue rolling until the seam seals and you have a long strand about 20 inches long, or a length that fits your baking sheet. Repeat with the other 2 pieces of dough.

4. Join the 3 strands together at one end and start to braid them. Try to keep your braiding fairly loose to leave room for the dough to rise. Once you reach the ends of the strands, tuck them under themselves and move the challah to your lined baking sheet. Cover with the dish towel and leave to proof for about 30 minutes until doubled in size. Meanwhile, preheat your oven to 400°F.

5. Brush the challah with egg wash very lightly to prevent releasing any air, then scatter with sesame seeds, then bake for 30–35 minutes until browned on top.

6. Take out of the oven and let cool completely on a wire rack before cutting it — I know it's very hard to resist the intoxicating challah aroma, but this is very important, as the dough still needs to set. So be patient because it will be worth it!

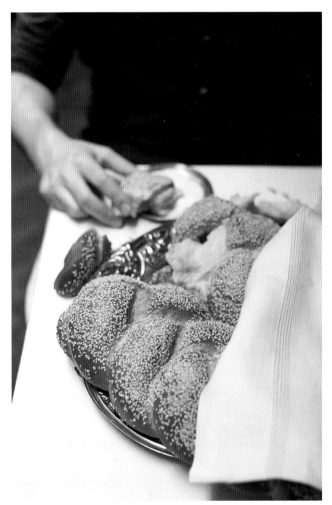

Jerusalem bagel

Makes 4 small bagels

* 2 cups strong white bread
  flour, plus extra for dusting
* 1 tbsp fresh yeast (or about 1 tsp
  fast-acting dried yeast)
* 2 tbsp granulated sugar
* 1 cup tepid water
* 2 pinches of salt
* 1 tbsp olive oil, plus extra for
  oiling and brushing
* 2¾ cups sesame seeds,
  for coating

Every Saturday while I was growing up, my family used to drive to a different part of Israel, and the most vivid part of those memories for me is the ride home. On the side of the road, just before we reached Jerusalem, there was always a man selling bagels with a small sachet made from old newspaper filled with za'atar. This signaled to me that we were close to home. Nowadays you can only find this treat in the Old City, and even though 20 years have passed, you can still get the za'atar in newspaper sachets.

1. In the bowl of an electric mixer fitted with a dough hook, or in a mixing bowl if making by hand, mix the flour and yeast, then add the sugar and water and knead on a low speed for about 4 minutes until a dough starts to form.

2. Add the salt and oil and knead for another 4 minutes. It will look as though the dough is separating, but don't worry, as in time it will absorb all the oil and come together.

3. Transfer the dough to an oiled bowl, cover with a clean dish towel and let rise at room temperature for about an hour or until tripled in size.

4. Divide the dough into quarters and roll each into a ball. Place on a floured work surface, cover with the dish towel and leave to rest for another 30 minutes. Meanwhile, preheat your oven to 475°F and line a baking sheet with parchment paper.

5. It's time to shape your bagels! The traditional shape is a long oval with a hole in the middle, but you can also make round bagels. Take one piece of dough, flatten it slightly with your hands to let the air out and then roll it tightly to make a short strand. Continue rolling to elongate it until you have a rope-like strand about 20 inches long. Repeat with the rest of the dough balls.

6. Bring either end of each strand together to create an oval shape and give them a little roll to help them stay attached.

7. To coat the dough, you will need 1 tub filled with water and another tub of sesame seeds, both big enough to accommodate a dough shape. Now take each dough shape in turn and dip in the water for no more than a second, making sure it gets wet all over, then place it in the sesame tub and coat on all sides (just like coating a schnitzel).

8. When all 4 dough shapes are coated with sesame seeds, place them on the lined baking sheet and bake for 10 minutes.

9. As soon as they come out of the oven, brush them with olive oil. If you're not going to eat them all on the same day you made them, you can freeze them in a sealed freezer bag or container.

Kreplach

Makes 25–30 dumplings

Kreplach are filled dough dumplings: the Ashkenazi Jewish version of Italian ravioli, Chinese wonton or Russian pelmeni. There are two different methods of making the dough, the most common involving simply mixing flour, water and eggs together. The second approach, which I prefer, is where the dough is cooked in a similar way to French choux pastry, and once I'd tried it, I never looked back. The dough is fairly soft, so you can easily roll it out using a rolling pin, but I like to use a pasta machine because it makes the task easy, and you get a neater result as the dough is an even thickness throughout. In either case, the secret is to not use too much flour — the more flour you add, the tougher the dumpling. Having said that, be relatively free with the flour, otherwise the dough will stick. Remember to stop rolling from time to time and check that it's not sticking to the work surface.

If you want to fry the finished kreplach in a pan, it's best to fold the dough in half to create half-moon shapes, whereas if you're planning on cooking them in a soup, you can go for the fancier look and make the tortellini shape.

---

* 1 cup water
* 1 tbsp olive oil
* ½ tbsp salt
* 2¼ cups all-purpose flour, plus extra for dusting
* 3 tbsp egg yolks (about 3–4, depending on the egg size)

---

1. To make the dough, bring the water, oil and salt to the boil in a large saucepan over a high heat — since we don't want the water to evaporate. Choose a bigger saucepan than you need, as you will be mixing the dough in it.

2. Add half the flour all at once and stir until the mixture starts to clump together into a dough.

3. Remove the pan from the heat, transfer the dough to the bowl of an electric mixer fitted with a dough hook and knead on a low speed for a minute to cool it down slightly. If making by hand, transfer the dough to a mixing bowl and knead the dough in the same way, wearing heat-resistant gloves, as the dough is very hot at this stage.

4. Add the rest of the flour and then the egg yolks, and continue kneading for about 2–3 minutes until all the ingredients are well combined. If using an electric mixer, you can take the dough out and knead it a little with your hands, which will help it to form into a nice ball of dough.

5. Wrap the dough in plastic wrap and leave to rest in the fridge for at least a few hours, preferably overnight.

6. To make the kreplach, flour your work surface and roll out the dough to a thickness of 1⁄16–1⁄8 inch. Check from time to time that the dough is not sticking to the surface, dusting with more flour as needed. If using a pasta machine, roll it out to setting number 3 or 4 (the settings vary with each machine), making sure that you keep dusting the dough with flour to prevent it sticking to the machine.

7. Use a cutter or an upturned glass to cut the dough into 3½-inch rounds.

8. For half-moon-shaped dumplings, place a heaping teaspoonful (or use a piping bag and pipe the equivalent amount) of filling in the center of each round. Fold the round in half, ensuring that you don't trap any air inside the dumpling, otherwise once in the cooking liquid, the air will turn to steam and burst through the dough. Press the edges together to seal so that they won't open during cooking — the dough usually sticks to itself, but if it needs a little help, you can brush a bit of water over the problematic area to help the dough edges hold together.

9. For the tortellini shape, draw the 2 corners of each half-moon in to meet and press them together.

10. Your kreplach are now ready to cook (see p. 191), or freeze them for later.

A LIFE IN KITCHENS

by Yossi "Papi" Elad

When I was six years old, I knew I would be a cook. I inherited my passion for good food from my father. I can remember as a little boy standing next to him on a tiny bench in the kitchen, helping prepare meals for our family and friends. On our farm we had fresh milk from our neighbor's cows, eggs from our chickens and vegetables from our garden, which gave me respect for ingredients.

My cooking comes first from the heart because I love people; the people I cook for are no less important than the food I cook.

Never think of recipes as sacrosanct — they are creations of human beings, so use your imagination. Be inspired by the recipes in this book and other cookbooks, but make them your own. That is what I do; I respect other chefs but I need to cook my way. A brilliant artist once said something that I also now use: "Great chefs copy, genius chefs steal!"

In 2009 the great chef Uri Navon (master of the universe), the TV star Assaf Granit (known by everyone in Israel) and I opened Machneyuda near the Machane Yehuda market. Two months later, the lines of customers were endless.

It took us five years to get to London, and it began after Zoe and Layo came to see us at Machneyuda. We arrived here with more questions than answers, but with a vision and a simple idea: to bring ourselves and our philosophy and cook the food we know and love. The Palomar is a place of hospitality. We want our customers to feel like they are visiting us at our home: that's what we teach our staff.

We are trying to establish a new and modern cuisine, yet the Israeli kitchen, though young, is based on long-standing traditions. Our grandmothers taught me many of the secrets I know.

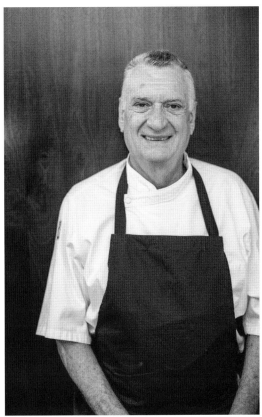

Yossi "Papi" Elad at The Palomar, 2015

THE PALOMAR DICTIONARY

by Tomer Amedi

Before I moved to London, I was daunted more than anything by the prospect of a new language. I remember trying out my (terrible) English accent during service at Machneyuda, going for classic British restraint, driving the team crazy… I really wanted to avoid turning up in the UK and making a fool of myself. But by our second night at The Palomar, I realized that the truer I am to myself, the better my team gets along and the more fun it is for everyone. Over time, cooks started joining us from a whole host of different countries, and naturally a polyglot mishmash of Palomar slang emerged. We have had some very funny "lost in translation" moments. Poor Pietro spent a long time eagerly greeting everyone with, "Yemacha esmack," grinning warmly, only to learn that it means, "Your name shall be vanished from history." Our kitchen slang has evolved from Hebrew, English, Arabic, Italian and god only knows what else. So here is our unique Palomar kitchen lexicon.

Balagan — "A big mess" in Hebrew slang. For example: "What is this balagan?! Who spilt sauce on my station?"

Chaptcha — "A little bit" in Kurdish. For example: "Don't be so tirchio; put chaptcha more salt."

Ciccio/Ciccia — "Fatso" in Italian, this is an affectionate name but can also be a bit of a tease. For example: "Ciccia, pass me the knife," or "Hey, Ciccio, are you going to leave any pasta for me?"

Kapara — An affectionate name Moroccan mums usually use when calling for their kids, meaning "My redemption." For example: "Kapara, pass me the saucepan."

Ken — Hebrew for "Yes."

Khawdash — "New" in Hebrew, this is what we call out every time there's a new ticket for an order. For example: "Khawdash, Table 24, 2 polenta, 1 shakshukit, 3 pork."

Kibalti — "Got it!" For example: "Chef, 3 minutes for steak." "Kibalti, 3 minutes."

Lo — Hebrew for "No."

Sababa — "Cool" in Hebrew slang. For example: "Give me table 24, then 26, 30 and 31, Sababa?" "Sababa!"

Tirchio — "Tight-fisted" or "cheap" in Italian. For example: "Don't be so tirchio; put some more herbs on the plate."

Toda — "Thank you" in Hebrew. For example: "Kapara, pass me the blue chopping board," and then, "Toda, Kapara," "Sababa, chef."

Yalla — "Hurry up." For example: "Yalla yalla, finish the ticket."

The Palomar team

Chef Amedi aka Tomer; Papi aka
the Godfather; Thomas aka "Done Chef"
Youell; NinoNinoNino; Dario
aka Scooby Doo; Jefferson aka
Josperson; Terry aka Mother Teresa;
Ayesha aka Jordanian Amy Winehouse;
Tom "Eggsy" Oliver (not the son of);
Stavros aka The Greek Josh Hartnett;
Eyal "Shpitz" Jagermann; Alex "the
Mensch" Spitzer; Shay–but not so;
Emanuele "Meme;" Ariana; Helen
and the timer; Uriya 1,2,3 dibuk; Mitz
the boyfriend, or Shauli or Shaul; Flo
Ryder; Kipper aka Kip Kip; Pietro
aka Picasso; Daniele aka Robo Cop;
Christian kapara; Yael aka Yaeli Mami;
Kader aka Junior; Tulisa; Spanky;
Jason; Kasia; Marco; Michael; John;
Tom; Giuseppe; Nick; Laurent; James;
Gary; Olivier; Omer; Olga; Laszlo;
Kirsty; David; Esther; William; Sahar;
Laura; Louisa; Meagan; Cecilia;
Aline; Fin; Layo; Zoe; "Alice Palace"
Bradford; Princessa Andreina; Julie
"McWonderful" Parland; Amy; Paul B
and Maxine.

DEDICATION

This book is dedicated to all the people who have worked so hard to make
The Palomar the restaurant it has become, and to you, the public, for joining
us in this journey, and allowing us the opportunity for such creative freedom
every day and every night.

AUTHORS' ACKNOWLEDGMENTS

The Palomar would like to thank our wonderful friend and agent, Zoe Ross.

The long-suffering team (as a result of having us as authors) at Octopus especially
Stephanie Jackson, Sybella Stephens, Caroline Brown and Jonathan Christie.

Helen Cathcart for her beautiful photography and her willingness to let Tomer
"art direct" some dishes against her better judgment.

And finally Solène, Nichole and Caz at Here Design — pure magic!

And definitely not last, except in this instance, Alice Bradford (too many job titles
to list here, and we are way over our word count) but without her tireless attention
to detail, this book would be full of poor grammar, mistakes and bad photos!

Publishing Director: Stephanie Jackson
Managing Editor: Sybella Stephens
Copy Editor: Jo Richardson
Creative Director: Jonathan Christie
Design and Art Direction: Here Design
Photographer: Helen Cathcart
Senior Production Manager: Peter Hunt
Production Controller: Meskerem Berhane